What **Philosophers** Think

What Philosophers Think

Edited by Julian Baggini and Jeremy Stangroom

continuum
LONDON • NEW YORK

Continuum
The Tower Building
11 York Road
London SE1 7NX
www.continuumbooks.com

15 East 26th Street
New York
NY 10010

Reprinted 2003

British Library Cataloguing-in-Publication Data
A catalogue record for this book is available from the British Library.

ISBN: 0-8264-6754-7 (hardback)
      0-8264-6180-8 (paperback)

Typeset by BookEns Ltd, Royston, Herts.
Printed and bound in Great Britain by Biddles Ltd, *www.biddles.co.uk*

Contents

Acknowledgements

Special thanks to Ophelia Benson for her tremendous help editing the interviews. Thanks also to Tristan Palmer and Rowan Wilson at Continuum; and to Sophie Cox and Katherine Savage for their diligence and patience.

Introduction

What Philosophers Think

If you want to know what philosophers think, you might suppose that the best thing to do is to read some of their books. However, there is one very good reason why this collection of interviews might be better equipped to satisfy your curiosity. Put simply, in their published works, philosophers do not tend to tell you exactly what they think about a range of issues. Rather, they only tell you what they have original and compelling arguments to believe about a generally narrow range of topics. This contrast, and its significance, requires a little explaining.

For starters, we need to be clear about how philosophy works. Philosophy is sometimes thought to be about ideas or theories. This is true only in the way that gambling and business are both about money. Money is what is transacted in gambling and business, but you don't understand what trade and business are, and the differences between them, if you only know they involve money exchanges. Similarly, philosophy's currency is ideas, but then so is it the currency of science and religion. What makes the difference is how the currency is traded.

What regulates the flow of ideas in philosophy is rational argumentation. Exactly what makes an argument rational is itself a philosophical question, but in general it is that any conclusions reached are based upon a combination of good evidence, good reasoning and self-evident basic principles of logic. (The 'evidence' philosophy draws upon is not usually the special data of science, but the kind of evidence which is available to all. These are facts which are established by everyday experience or established science. In this way, there is no special evidence-base for philosophy.)

So, when philosophers 'go to market' and publish, what they set out are not all their ideas. They only trade in what they believe they have strong evidential and argumentative grounds to assert. They do not set out 'what they think' but what they have good reasons to believe. This is what gives philosophical work its value. If philosophers just wrote about what they thought then we would have a surfeit of ideas and nothing to help tell us which are right and which are wrong.

This is a point which a lot of 'amateur' philosophers (i.e. philosophers working independently outside of academia) are wont to miss. Too often they rush to put all of their ideas on paper and either fail to back them up with good arguments or offer cursory, inadequate justifications. They are then surprised that no serious publisher is interested in accepting their work. Academic philosophers are helped in this regard by the fact that their work is closely scrutinized and criticized by their peers. Independent philosophers often have to rely entirely on self-evaluation and it is very hard to be a good self-critic. This, rather than any lack of ability or prejudice, is probably the main reason why so little decent philosophy is produced outside of academia.

However, although this filtering of ideas serves an important function, it does rob of us some interesting material. The filter applies across the board to all philosophers, regardless of their abilities. So even the best philosophers of each generation tend only to publish those ideas for which they have 'industry standard' arguments. It is true that publishers will cut the elite a little slack and some philosophical 'superstars' do publish work which is not backed up by generally expected standards of argument, much to their lesser-known peers' chagrin. But these are exceptions. In general, even the top philosophers adhere to the rule which states: don't tell us what you think; tell us what you can provide strong, rational arguments to support.

In general this is a good thing. But there are several reasons why, sometimes at least, we might want to take a slightly broader view and see what philosophers think about things for which they haven't necessarily got strong philosophical arguments.

One such reason is that there can be little doubt that philosophers, as individual human beings, bring something of themselves to their professional work. The idea that philosophy is played out in some impersonal, purely rational realm is a myth which confuses philosophy's aspirations for its actuality. Read any autobiography by a philosopher and it becomes evident that their thought is at least in part shaped by their personalities. For instance, Quine as a toddler enjoyed 'the reduction of the unfamiliar to the familiar', while the young Feyerabend assumed the world was a magical, mysterious place. It is implausible to suppose that the mature philosophies of these thinkers just so happen to chime with these largely pre-reflective cognitive tendencies.

In their published works, philosophers exert a great deal of control over what they write. This often has the effect of suppressing their personalities to the extent that little or nothing of them shines through. In an interview setting, the philosopher has less control and as a result more of their self comes across. This is not something that can be pinned down to particular sentences or phrases, nor is it usually down to overtly autobiographical references. It is rather that in various, subtle ways, the self will out in an interview where it may not in a monograph.

For example, in the interviews with Peter Vardy and Russell Stannard, one gets a much greater sense of the role which religious faith plays in their thought and life than one does in their own writings. In their books, Vardy and Stannard present and discuss arguments for and against religious belief and although you know which side they come down on, it is hard to determine just how significant these arguments are for them. In the interviews the truth is much more transparent: the arguments that they make just aren't that important for their faith. They live by their religious convictions, and the arguments for or against the existence of God, for example, do not alter these convictions. It is nice if their beliefs find rational support, but no problem if they don't.

This is a very interesting finding because it tells you something, not at all evident in the standard texts of the philosophy of religion, about the way in which life and thought interact for many believers. It makes one reconsider the true function of arguments for the existence of God and it certainly problematizes the widespread belief that these arguments can or should actually inform what people believe about God.

This example also shows something about how interviews are a very useful way of getting into metaphilosophy – the study of the nature and methods of philosophy. The metaphilosophical framework within which a thinker operates is rarely made explicit. In an interview, however, parts of this framework can come to the fore. Many of the interviews in this book touch upon metaphilosophical themes. Hilary Putnam, for example, talks about the role of judgement in philosophy and the need to acknowledge that any given piece of philosophy is done by a person, an individual human being. John Searle's interview explores many of the ways in which rational justifications are constrained and which principles a philosopher must work from in order to avoid the 'preposterous'. In an interview, a thinker can stand back from their work and tell us something about how they do it, whereas in their published work they are usually just interested in getting on with doing it.

Interviews also enable the philosophers to explore some of the links in their work. For instance, Janet Radcliffe Richards makes some interesting observations about the continuities between her earlier work on feminism and her more recent work on Darwinism and bioethics. These links are not self-evident, but once they are explained they highlight some important features of Radcliffe

Richards's approach to philosophy (thus again bringing out some metaphilosophical points).

We can also often see what is really fundamental for a philosopher. In the interview with Peter Singer, for example, it quickly becomes evident that he is not very interested in theoretical questions of ethics which don't have a direct bearing on practical morality. This shows us what Singer's fundamental convictions about ethics are: that theory is not of interest in itself and that practical guidance is moral philosophy's goal.

In short, interviews can show the broader picture. They enable us to stand back from the detailed arguments of philosophers in their published works and see the various background beliefs, convictions and assumptions that provide the usually unseen context for their philosophizing. They also enable us to see how the philosophers themselves see their published work fitting in with their wider commitments. As Peter Vardy says in his interview, 'One isn't a philosopher all one's life, one has to stake one's life.' As philosophers, the interviewees in this book have to balance arguments and assess which are stronger. As people, they often have to come down on one side or another, whether or not they have satisfactory philosophical arguments to help them decide. It can be telling to see which options they plump for.

What's a Philosopher?

The title of this book may be thought to be misleading, since several of the interviewees are not philosophers by profession. Alan Sokal and Russell Stannard are both physicists, Edward O. Wilson a naturalist, Richard Dawkins a zoologist and Don Cupitt primarily a theologian. However, the intellectual realm is not as neat as standard academic nomenclature would suggest. Philosophy is a subject which crosses borders, and full-time philosophers do not have a monopoly on the subject. In each interview with a 'non-philosopher' here, the subject matter is work that the thinkers have done which is primarily philosophical in nature. All have strayed into philosophy, by accident or design, and so have, however temporarily, become philosophers. This is why we see no incongruity between the book's title and its contents.

This does, however, invite the question as to what exactly makes something philosophy, as opposed to theology, sociology or cultural theory, for instance. The question is too large to be properly answered here. But we can gesture towards an answer by pointing out why our non-philosophers ended up doing philosophy. In Sokal's case, the answer is simple: Sokal set out to parody and criticize certain forms of philosophy and so is something of a philosophical gatecrasher. Richard Dawkins's ideas necessarily invite philosophical questions about things like determinism, reductionism and scientism. Wilson's *Consilience* project is through and through philosophical in that it is predicated upon claims about the nature and scope of knowledge. Stannard entered philosophical territory when he set out to see if the existence of God could be established using standard scientific techniques. This leads one into issues about the nature of religious belief and how it can or should be justified. Cupitt ventures into philosophy because his writings on religion hinge on questions about what it means to believe in God and whether or not the objects of belief have to be things which exist independently of human minds.

In all these cases the thinkers were drawn to general questions about the nature and justification of knowledge, belief, existence and key concepts such as free will, determinism, God and truth. These are trademark philosophical questions because they deal with general and fundamental questions about things which we do not think can be understood by scientific, empirical enquiry alone. The fact that thinkers outside philosophy are often drawn to such questions shows how philosophy is in some sense the fundamental intellectual discipline. It deals with those theoretical and abstract issues that are left unresolved by the particular methods of the natural and social sciences, but which those sciences themselves rest upon. Once we see this, we can understand how it is no surprise to see 'non-philosophers' doing some philosophy themselves from time to time.

The Range of Topics

The range of topics discussed in the book is partly a result of historical accident: these just happen to be the themes that each issue of *The Philosophers' Magazine* focused on and which provided the original *raisons d'être* of the interviews. However, seeing what topics were chosen to be covered does reveal something about the interest and concerns of contemporary academic philosophy: *The Philosophers' Magazine* only reflects what is happening in the philosophical world.

It is certainly no coincidence that three of the interviews have Darwinian themes. Philosophical interest in Darwin grew enormously in the 1990s, spurred on by the work of the Darwin@LSE programme at the London School of Economics' Centre for the Philosophy of the Natural and Social Sciences. The programme is led by Helena Cronin, one of our interviewees, and it was a Darwin@LSE event which provided the occasion for Peter Singer to give the lecture which provided the focus for his interview.

This interest in Darwin is in fact part of a wider trend in Anglo-American philosophy: the growth in naturalism. Naturalism is the broad term given to a range of approaches in philosophy which have in common the attempt to root philosophical explanations in the functioning of the natural world. Naturalism's godfather is David Hume, whose moral philosophy is perhaps most obviously naturalistic. For Hume, we do not understand our feelings for right and wrong by forming rational arguments for morality. We can only understand morality when we see it as a kind of instinct, a feeling instilled in us by nature. Fast-forward two centuries and we can see how attempts to explain our moral instinct in Darwinian terms are continuous with Hume's project.

There is now no area of philosophy in which naturalistic explanations are not offered. Like all movements in philosophy, it has plenty of critics. Whereas proponents see it as an attempt to root good philosophy in good science, critics say it is often both bad philosophy and bad science. Readers can make a preliminary judgement for themselves on the basis of the evidence served up by the interviews here.

Science is another theme covered by this book. What is interesting here is that none of the interviewees in this section are full-time philosophers. This is telling. In recent years scientists and those interested in science have shown a great deal of interest in the philosophical issues that surround science, such as the status of scientific theories, the nature of scientific truth and the borderline between science and other forms of belief or knowledge. At the same time, academic philosophy of science has not been enjoying a purple patch. There are few heavyweights in the field – certainly no giants.

This should perhaps not surprise us. There is often a mismatch between the areas of philosophy which are of greatest wider concern and those which are thriving within academia. The philosophy of language, for example, occupied pole position in academic philosophy for a long time without ever catching the imagination of those outside it. Our interviews on that theme investigate the reasons why the topic remains stubbornly unsexy. With science the asymmetry runs the other way: academic philosophy of science is at a low point, while public interest in the philosophical issues that surround science is at a high.

There are several interviews which are grouped together under the title *Philosophy and Society*. Although philosophy is often removed from the concerns of everyday life, it never entirely loses touch with them. Issues of morality, justice and art are perennial themes in philosophy and perennial concerns of society. It is natural that they are represented here.

The philosophy of religion is also well-represented. This is a topic which always generates plenty of reaction from readers of *The*

Philosophers' Magazine and it is probably reader interest which has led to it being covered so well here. However, as with the philosophy of science, too much should not be read into this. In academic philosophy, religion is not a core concern. Indeed, there is evidence that academic philosophers are less religious on the whole than the general population and most are left cold by the traditional debates of the philosophy of religion. Here we have an example of how philosophy can remain of interest even when it is not new. The debates in the philosophy of religion are tired and sterile for most philosophers, but they remain pertinent for those not immersed in the subject.

Finally, the branch of philosophy with the most exotic name – metaphysics – also finds its home in these pages. The most fundamental metaphysical issue of all – the nature of reality – is discussed twice, while one of the oldest problems in philosophy – that of free will – also shows its face.

What we do not see here as the particular focus of any interview is the theory of knowledge (epistemology). This is arguably the most fundamental area of philosophy, since it concerns the question of what knowledge is and what we can know. It would be wrong to say the theme is entirely absent, however. It runs through the Edward O. Wilson and Russell Stannard interviews, but in specific and largely non-standard forms. And it lurks in the background of most of the other discussions, the Banquo at a banquet, uninvited but there to stay. Readers are advised to look out for this ghostly presence while reading the book. The question of what we can know and how we can know it is implicitly raised on countless occasions, as are some possible answers.

The Origins of the Interviews

All these interviews were published in their original form in *The Philosophers' Magazine* between 1998 and 2002. However, in preparing them for this anthology we have not simply repackaged them. Every interview has been revised and in many cases they have been extended to include exchanges that were left out of the magazine due to length restrictions. We have also standardized the format to a large extent and have been able to give more background to the interviews in order to contextualize them. The interviews have also been back to the interviewees who have often taken the opportunity to tidy up their own words while admirably resisting the temptation to rewrite history.

The result is, we hope, a series of interviews that are of much longer-lasting interest than most journalistic articles.

1 Darwin's Legacy

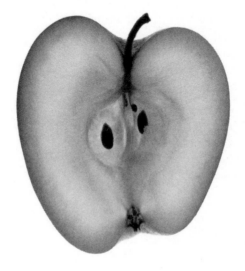

1 Darwin and Ethics

Peter Singer

The story of moral philosophy in the English-speaking world in the late twentieth century is captured in miniature by the story of Peter Singer. Arriving in Oxford as a postgraduate student in 1969 Singer entered a world on the cusp of change as a man on the brink of change. Moral philosophy had for many years been a dry and lifeless affair. Meta-ethics – the study of the nature of moral judgements – had been its almost exclusive concern, while issues in applied ethics – what we should actually do – were marginalized. The war in Vietnam and the civil rights movement had shaken this status quo in the United States and changes were also becoming evident in Britain.

Singer arrived in Oxford with no particular interest in animal rights. But, as he reports in *Between the Species*, encounters with lecturers and contemporaries such as Ros and Stan Godlovitch, Richard Keshen and Richard Ryder began to change his thinking. Singer had started out on an intellectual journey from which he would emerge as the best-known philosophical proponent of animal rights of his time.

The breakthrough was *Animal Liberation*, published in 1975. In it, Singer argued that it follows from the fact that animals have awareness and feel pain that we have a moral obligation to guard their welfare, which in practice means virtually no vivisection and almost total vegetarianism. But note the qualifications. Singer has always argued strictly from utilitarian principles – we must do what most satisfies the preferences of sentient creatures and avoid what frustrates these preferences. The desire to follow through on this principle consistently is probably what has generated the most controversy. For hard-line animal rights campaigners it means he doesn't go far enough. More controversial, however, have been Singer's arguments concerning human life. Singer has argued that, since it is sentience or consciousness which gives life value, the life of an unborn child, newly born infant or very severely mentally handicapped child is worth less than that of many animals. His willingness to make these claims and maintain the consistency of his position has led to boycotts, protests and countless accusations of being 'evil' or a 'Nazi'.

When I met Peter Singer, he looked a very tired man. On a lecture tour of Britain, his notoriety had once again resulted in weeks of media scrutiny, misrepresentation and criticism, which seem to have taken their toll.

Singer came to England to talk about 'A Darwinian Left', but no sooner had he stepped off the plane than the *Daily Express* was reviving the old controversy over Singer's view that in certain circumstances it may be better to end the life of a very severely handicapped baby in a humane way, rather than use all modern medicine can do to let it live a painful and often brief life. Singer tried to defend himself on Radio 4's *Today* programme, but in such a brief news item, his calm reasoning was always likely to have less impact than the emotive pleas of his opponent.

So once again, what Singer really wanted to say was overshadowed by his reputation. Which is a pity, because his London School of Economics lecture, *A Darwinian Left?*, which formed the centrepiece of his visit, saw Singer challenging a rather different taboo: the exclusion from left-wing thought of the ideas of Charles Darwin.

Singer argues that the Left's utopianism has failed to take account of human nature, because it has denied there is such a thing as a human nature. For Marx, it is the 'ensemble of social relations' which makes us the people we are, and so, as Singer points out, 'It follows from this belief that if you can change the "ensemble of social relations", you can totally change human nature.'

The corruption and authoritarianism of so-called Marxist and communist states in this century is testament to the naïveté of this view. As the anarchist Bakunin said, once even workers are given absolute power, 'they represent not the people but themselves … Those who doubt this know nothing at all about human nature.'

But what then is this human nature? Singer believes the answer comes from Darwin. Human nature is an evolved human nature. To understand why we are the way we are and the origins of ethics, we have to understand how we have evolved not just physically, but mentally. Evolutionary psychology, as it is known, was the intellectual growth industry of the last decade of the millennium, though not without its detractors.

Singer argues that if the Left takes account of evolutionary psychology, it will be better able to harness that understanding of human nature to implement policies which have a better chance of success. In doing so, two fallacies about evolution have to be cleared up. First of all, we have evolved not to be ruthless proto-capitalists, but to 'enter into mutually beneficial forms of co-operation'. It is the evolutionary psychologist's explanation of how 'survival of the fittest' translates into co-operative behaviour which has been, arguably, its greatest success. Secondly, there is the 'is/ought' gap. To say a certain type of behaviour has evolved is not to say it is morally right. To accept a need to understand how our minds evolved is not to endorse every human trait with an evolutionary origin.

When I spoke to Peter Singer, I wanted to get clearer about what he thinks Darwinism can do to help us understand ethics. Singer is a preference utilitarian, which means he thinks the morally right action is that which has the consequences of satisfying the preferences of the greatest number of people. Singer seems now to be saying that the importance of Darwinism is that if we take it into account, we will be better at producing the greatest utility: the maximum satisfaction of people's preferences.

'That's my philosophical goal,' acknowledges Singer. 'I was speaking more broadly for anyone who shares a whole range of values. You don't have to be a preference utilitarian. But I think it would be true generally that anyone who has views about how society should end up will have a better chance to achieve that if they understand the Darwinian framework of human nature.'

Singer also argues that Darwinism has a useful debunking effect, in that if you accept it, certain other positions are fatally undermined. For example, the idea that God gave Adam, and by proxy, us, dominion over the animal kingdom is a view 'thoroughly refuted by the theory of evolution'.

'A lot of the impetus for a divine command theory comes from the idea: "where could ethics come from?",' he explains. 'It's something totally different, out of this world, so therefore you have to assume we're talking about the will of God or something. Once you have a Darwinian understanding of how ethics can emerge, you absolutely don't have to assume that, but it's still possible to assume it. It's really the "I have no need of the hypothesis" rather than "that hypothesis is hereby refuted".'

The question of how far evolution can help us understand the origin of ethics is perhaps the most contentious part of evolutionary psychologists' claims in general and Singer's thesis in particular. Singer believes Darwinian theory gives us an understanding of the origin of ethics, because, for example, it gives an evolutionary explanation of how reciprocity came to be. Put crudely, if you model the survival prospects for different kinds of creatures with different ways of interacting with others – from serial exploiters to serial co-operators and every shade in between – it turns out that the creatures who thrive in the long run are those that adopt a strategy called 'tit for tat'. This means that they always seek to co-operate with others, but withdraw that co-operation as soon as they are taken advantage of. Because this is the attitude which increases the survival value of a species, it would seem to follow that humans have evolved an in-built tendency to co-operation, along with a tendency to withdraw that co-operation if exploited. Hence, it is argued, an essential feature of ethics – reciprocity – is explained by evolution.

But when we give an evolutionary explanation of how reciprocity came to be, we're only describing evolved behaviour, and it is quite clear that what we think ethics is now goes beyond a mere description of our evolved behaviour. It concerns how we ought to behave, not just how we do. So how historically or logically is that gap between 'is' and 'ought' bridged?

'It's not bridged historically at all,' replies Singer. 'Of any culture and people you can describe their ethic, but that remains entirely on the level of description. "The Inuit people do this and this and this, the British people do that and that and that." You can describe that ethic but you don't get from the answer to "what ought I to do?". So the gap is a logical one and it just arises from the fact that when we seek to answer the question, "What ought I to do?" we're asking for a prescription, we're not asking for a description. Any description of existing morals in our culture or the origins of morals is not going to enable us to deduce what we ought to do.'

But, I insist, doesn't then evolution merely explain the descriptive part of how certain behaviours came to be? It doesn't really explain our ethics, it explains social codes, rules of social conduct. If ethics is a prescriptive field distinct from a descriptive one, how do evolutionary explanations of how merely described behaviour comes to be explain how ethics came to be?

'I think in a way that's so obvious that it doesn't need any explanation,' retorts Singer. 'That's just that we have the capacity to make choices and that we make judgements which are prescriptive, first person, second person or third person judgements. So, in a way, that is not what I'm trying to explain the origins of, although you can see how if you add it to the kinds of accounts I've given, and since we have language and we are social animals, you can see why we end up talking about these things and discussing them. We know that we do that, and that's a process you would expect beings, once they had a certain degree of language, faced with these choices, to do.'

The question is important, because some prominent workers in the area of decision-theory and evolution argue that evolution explains how it comes to be that we have social rules and that in fact understanding these origins shows us that there's no extra moral dimension to these things. They are merely evolved and we deceive ourselves if we think there is an ethical dimension.

I try to probe this apparent gap between evolution and ethics by considering two of Singer's examples of how our ethics must account for our evolved human nature. If we take into account the fact that we feel more protective towards our own offspring than to children in general, it's a good rule that parents should take care of their children because there's a greater chance it will increase the general happiness. On the other hand, the double standard towards female and male sexual behaviour, even though it may have an evolutionary explanation, is something that should not be tolerated. I put it to Singer that it follows that the moral judgements we're going to make are going to be of the sort, 'If the evolved behaviour is going to lead to the morally desirable result, follow it, and if the evolved behaviour does not lead to the morally desirable result, don't follow it.' So isn't the observation of what has evolved going to drop out of the equation? It's not going to feed at all directly into what our moral rules are going to be.

Singer's answer reveals more precisely the limited, but important, role he believes Darwinian explanations play in our ethics. 'I think the Darwinian is going to alert us to what rules are going to work and what rules are going to meet a lot of resistance, and I think we have to bear that in mind. But always there's a trade off between how important the values are to us and the strength of the evolved tendency in our natures.'

Given Singer's willingness to challenge established views, it is perhaps surprising that he still talks in terms of the Left and Right, particularly as it seems his conception of the Left is a long way from any traditional view. Singer characterizes the Left as being concerned with eliminating the sufferings of others and of the oppressed. A lot of people on the Left would consider that quite a diluted view of the Left, which has something to do with common ownership. So is it still useful to maintain the label 'the Left'?

'The label's kind of there to stay,' replies Singer. 'It's been there so long. We're not about to get rid of it. You would have to be rather far on the Left now to think that a lot of common ownership is a good idea, beyond some major utilities. I wouldn't say the Left ought to be committed to common ownership. Common ownership is possibly a means to achieving the goals of the Left. That debate should continue. But I wouldn't say it was a prerequisite for being part of the Left.'

Pushed further on this, Singer simply replies, 'I think there's a lot less to the Left/Right distinction than there was, undoubtedly.' The answer may seem brusque, but it reflects where the locus of Singer's concerns lies. Singer is moved and motivated by moral practice, and any debate in moral philosophy which does not directly relate to how we are to live does not interest him. Moral theory is not of interest to him for its own sake, nor are theoretical debates about the scope of concepts.

Singer may feel that his new take on Darwin ought to have been the main focus of his visit to London. But aside from Singer the academic philosopher, there is also Singer the campaigner and polemicist. If the media have focused on other things, it is at least partly due to Singer's own outspokenness about issues that matter to him.

One of the first controversies to blow up in the press during Singer's visit was his withdrawal of a lecture he was due to give at the King's Centre for Philosophy because of its sponsorship by Shell UK, and his very public letter to the *Guardian* explaining why.

Singer's reason for pulling out is that, 'I did not really want to appear on a programme that says "supported by Shell" and is seen as therefore promoting the idea that Shell is a good corporate citizen. It's not that I'm against taking corporate money under any circumstances. I think there are some circumstances in which I would take it, but I think that you always have to be careful about taking corporate money. At present Shell's record, particularly in Nigeria, is really lamentable. I think that you can see a connection between the money that is going here [to the King's Centre] and the profits made out of the extraction of oil in Nigeria, with all of the consequences that has for the Ogoni people, both in terms of environmental damage to their land, and the way in which Shell revenues support the Nigerian dictatorship, which is one of the most oppressive around. So I just didn't want to be part of that.'

Interestingly, at one recent environmental ethics conference, at which the Shell issue in particular was in the forefront of people's minds, a lot of the people who gave consequentialist arguments at the conference actually came out in favour of taking the money, because they felt that the benefits of having the conference supported would outweigh the very marginal benefits that Shell would receive for having its logo in the corner of the posters. People said things like 'It's better this money is spent on a conference in environmental ethics, which should be discussed, than the money should go to a big billboard poster for Shell or something". What does Singer, as a consequentialist, make of this argument?

'The consequentialist could go both ways, I don't deny that. I don't think it's all that important to have another environmental ethics conference, frankly – there are plenty of environmental ethics conferences and discussions about environmental ethics around. There's certainly an argument about what else would happen to the money. But I think that in fact it's clear that as far as my gesture of refusing to take Shell's sponsorship – and it was a gesture, there's no doubt about it – it's had worthwhile consequences. What it's meant is that there's one lecture in my London programme that did not go ahead as sponsored, but in fact that was made up for by the fact that I gave a lecture organized at King's College by some students who were opposed to Shell's sponsorship. So people at King's still got to hear me give a lecture, if that's what they were interested in. By refusing and by writing a letter to the *Guardian* about my refusing to do so, there was a whole lot more discussion of the issue, so people have again become more aware that there is a real issue about corporate sponsorship and the question about Shell in particular has got aired. So, it seems to me that's clearly been a good thing. In other words, it's clear that I made the right decision on consequentialist grounds.

'But I think it's important that people enter some discussion, that it's not just a silent gesture, that I didn't give a lecture and no one ever heard about why I didn't.'

Singer is always very open in showing the full implications, consequences and ramifications of his viewpoint, which doesn't always make him popular. As a consequentialist, how does he feel about the argument that the best way to bring about a better society from a utilitarian point of view is not to advance complex utilitarian arguments but to appeal to more simple concepts?

'I think people are in different positions and different roles. For a political heavyweight involved in strategies for a political party to achieve office, it probably wouldn't be possible to be quite so open. But I think philosophers can have a role in clarifying people's thinking, with broader aims than simply saying "I want the political party with these views to get into office and do this and that".'

As an animal rights campaigner, I suggest, his roles perhaps are more mixed and I asked Singer whether he felt that being so open, and talking about the implications of his views on animals for mentally handicapped children, has had the effect of blunting his points on animal liberation, because people are inevitably not going to focus on his positive points about animals, they focus on the perceived negative implications for the sanctity of life.

'Maybe that's true. It's become a larger focus in recent years. I'm not quite sure why. Arguably, it was a mistake to write *Should the Baby Live?* back in 1985. But that's done now. I think the book's done some good in alerting people to the nature of that particular problem and making parents of the disabled able to discuss it more openly. I'm not going to deny that the conclusions still seem to be sound ones.

'I think you could say that politically it's been a mistake to accept invitations to debate it. What's happened in Britain over the last couple of weeks is that there was a rather silly article in the *Daily Express* that raised this issue, which probably should have been ignored, and I was called by the BBC for the *Today* programme and a lot of people heard that, so maybe it would have been more prudent to tell the BBC that I didn't really want to discuss that anymore and that wasn't what I was coming here to discuss this time.

'It's very hard because on the other hand some of the discussions were quite useful and it wasn't all silly stuff like the one on the *Today* programme. So you have to say, well, if it gets more attention, if more people read about my views, maybe some of them will think, "Well, this is not so silly and bad, maybe I should look at some of his books", and maybe more people will get involved in it. It's very hard to say.'

Singer is always going to be a controversial thinker because of his willingness to confront political and ethical issues without being constrained by current orthodoxy. His application of Darwin to left-wing thought is certainly not going to make him popular with the Right, but it is also likely to lose him some friends on the Left, just as his measured contribution to the issue of animal rights challenges society's attitudes while not going far enough to satisfy many activists.

Singer returned to his native Australia leaving behind a big question and a tentative answer. Can the scientific theories of Charles Darwin really contribute to our philosophical understanding of ethics? Singer has tried to show how it can, but this is a debate which clearly has a lot further to run.

Selected Bibliography

Animal Liberation (New York: New York Review/Random House, 1975)
Should the Baby Live?, with Helga Kuhse (Oxford: Oxford University Press, 1985)
Writings on an Ethical Life (London: HarperCollins, 2001)
A Darwinian Left (London: Weidenfeld and Nicolson, 1999)
One World: Ethics and Globalization (New Haven: Yale University Press, 2002)

2 Darwin, Nature and Hubris

Janet Radcliffe Richards

For a philosopher at the top of her profession, Janet Radcliffe Richards has surprisingly few published books to her name. Twenty years elapsed between her reputation-making debut *The Sceptical Feminist* in 1980 and the appearance of her second book, *Human Nature after Darwin*. However, she has been far from idle, and thanks to a steady stream of admired journal papers, Radcliffe Richards has maintained a respected position among her peers and a high public profile, frequently appearing on radio, television and in the national press.

Writing *The Sceptical Feminist* was a major turning point for Radcliffe Richards. 'The invitation to write it came out of the blue,' she recalls, 'and as I had been working on metaphysics and philosophy of science, and hardly thought about feminism, I still think it may have been a case of mistaken identity. But writing it changed my view about feminism.

'The interesting thing about writing the feminist book was that I hadn't regarded myself as a feminist before I started and I still ended up not liking what a lot of feminists were doing but I realized that women had a systematic and serious complaint. When I started I just thought there were a lot of men who didn't treat women well and it was just a matter of individuals.

'This was partly what underlay my reversion to my maiden name, and the adoption of my mother's maiden name of Radcliffe, which I now wish I'd had the nerve to adopt without keeping my maiden name as well. But more significantly, it turned my attention to the application of philosophy to moral and practical problems, which have been my concern ever since.'

The Sceptical Feminist exemplifies Radcliffe Richards's trademark approach to philosophy. She dissects arguments and analyses positions with clarity and precision, eschewing technicality but not at the expense of rigour. Rather like a modern-day Aristotle, her starting point is often the arguments and ideas that enjoy widespread support in contemporary society, rather than arcane positions held only by professional philosophers. This ensures that her work always has a practical resonance and is of interest to people beyond her profession.

Her second book was well worth the two-decade wait. Not only is it a much needed injection of calm sense into the ridiculously polarized 'Darwin Wars', it is also a wonderful masterclass in the elements of clear philosophical argument.

In the book, Richards outlines ways of conducting moral philosophical enquiry which is both refreshingly clear and effective, and potentially of great use in practical bioethics.

'I began to notice after some years that all the most striking arguments I was producing in moral and political contexts took a particular form, which I am trying to get more and more systematic,' she explains. 'Essentially it depends on first establishing a direction of onus of proof and then issuing a challenge on the basis of it. So if you can show that some policy has some clearly bad aspect, you take that as providing a *prima facie* case for rejecting it. You then challenge its supporters to produce an argument that defeats that presumption.

'This doesn't sound as though it could possibly get you anywhere,' she admits, 'because people will come back with counter arguments intended to do just that, and then you have to decide between the merits of the opposing cases in the usual way. But it is quite astonishing, once you get going in practical ethics, how many familiar lines of argument turn out to be straightforwardly spurious.

You often don't get as far as the difficult controversies, because the argument has already failed at a much simpler level.'

Radcliffe Richards is pleasantly surprised by how effective this apparently simple method is. 'It's amazing how many familiar views you can dispose of in this way, because most argument in ordinary life seems to work on the basis of starting with the conclusion you want to defend and then inventing a justification for it. This gives philosophers a potential field day, because arguments constructed that way round frequently contain mistakes of logic that nobody could possibly have made in a context where they did not already believe the conclusion.'

Human Nature after Darwin provides ample evidence for the system's merits. In it, she ruthlessly demolishes the fatuous arguments put forward by both opponents and supporters of evolutionary psychology to defend claims such as the need to bar women from certain jobs, the acceptability of sexual double-standards, and the implications of Darwin for free will and responsibility.

The method's strength is also its simplicity. 'In a sense, I take myself to be doing baby-level philosophy,' she says. 'I'm not very interested in the kind of ethics which consists of manipulating high level theoretical counters.' This might seem an incredible claim, but Radcliffe Richards makes a plausible case that, if practical ethics can only be done in the light of advanced ethical theory, it is utterly doomed.

'If you have to get the meta-ethical framework in place before you have serious discussions of the ground-level, practical problems, you might as well give up on them. In medical ethics, for instance, there is nothing so useless as telling a doctor that if you're a Kantian you do this and if you're a utilitarian you do that, because what the doctor wants to know is what to do, and can't wait until utilitarians and Kantians have come to the end of their arguments. So the challenge is to see how many practical moral conclusions can be reached without settling the fundamentals of ethical theory.'

But why should this method be so effective, when it is by its own lights so simple? ('That's the trouble with philosophy. Once you get something clear it looks obvious,' she remarked.)

'The thing which gives so much scope for getting the philosophical needle in, is that people's real reasons for reaching their practical conclusions are so often not the ones they give in their arguments. I'm particularly interested in what happens when there are widespread intellectual changes – in world view, or political and moral principles – but people still have deep convictions about the way things ought to be that are left over from previous frameworks. When this happens people try to fudge a justification for the old convictions in terms of the new principles – and it hardly ever works. This is what happened with feminism. After the Enlightenment, the idea that people were born to a particular place in life gradually became unacceptable, but most people were still convinced of traditional ideas about the natural position of men and women. So they tried to justify these old beliefs in terms of the new political ideas – and ran straight into logical absurdities that they didn't even notice, because they were so convinced of both the old conclusion and the new premises. Exposing these absurdities forces into the open the unacceptable moral views that are really doing the work.'

So does she think that, in the field of practical ethics, a lot can be done with no more than clear thinking?

'I think that's the only hope for practical ethics at the moment,' she agrees. 'I'd love to sort out the meta-ethical problems, but for now I'm trying to see how much can be done with the minimal meta-ethical principle that wherever you have conflicting moral views, you effectively haven't got a view at all. A moral view is supposed to guide action, and if it gives conflicting instructions – really conflicting, not just saying that different possible actions are equally good or bad – there's something wrong. In practice people have masses of conflicting principles, which they take off the shelf when they need to defend their current intuitions about how we should act. But if you really care about working out what is good – as opposed to finding plausible ways of making yourself look and feel good – you need to confront the contradictions.'

This way of doing things requires a basis of agreement among the disputants about moral fundamentals. Hence there are, in theory, cases when progress may not be possible.

'For instance, I take it as morally fundamental that suffering is intrinsically bad. Some people deny this; and if they persist in this denial after clarification (they usually turn out to mean that suffering can sometimes be instrumentally good – which is a quite different matter) there may be nothing more that argument can do. And if people really don't think it is morally important to avoid or prevent suffering, I'm not sure what you can do with them except put them on a desert island with no people or animals, so that they can't do any harm.'

One fascinating feature of Radcliffe Richards's methodology is that it can result in psychological predictions. She illustrated this with an account of what happened when she made her first foray into bioethics, writing on abortion in *The Sceptical Feminist*, where in some ways she made use of a method she had not yet explicitly articulated.

'I got into bioethics by accident – just as I got into feminism by accident – through the abortion arguments in *The Sceptical Feminist*. I had started off with the presumption that abortion was not a feminist issue at all because it was just about the entitlements of the foetus. But this is where I first discovered, although I didn't diagnose it until later, this method of arguing by burden of proof and challenge. The argument was essentially that if you are going to recommend a policy with one intrinsically bad element – in this case forcing a woman to have a child she does not want – you need to provide a good reason.

'Of course it sounds easy to find a reason – the child is a full human being and you mustn't kill human beings – and then you are back in the area of familiar controversy. But that argument can't be used by people who think you should allow some abortions but not others. So I set about trying to find a coherent principle that might provide a distinction between allowable and prohibited abortions in liberal countries such as ours. And the only one I could find was punishing women for sex. It sounds preposterous, but I didn't reach it through any kind of feminist ideology. It just seemed to be the only principle that came anywhere near fitting the practice.

'Then what was interesting was the amount of empirical evidence that supported it, like the original policy of not giving anaesthetics during abortions. And there does seem to be a high correlation between opposition to abortion and disapproval of sexual freedom; I'd be very interested to see a systematic study of that. It astonished me. I was not expecting to find philosophical argument generating psychological hypotheses in this way. But I find it happens a lot. It has happened with the euthanasia debate, for instance. It takes some argument to show it, but I think the details of most anti-euthanasia attitudes can be coherently justified only by a deep assumption that suicide is wrong – probably because life belongs to God.'

I remarked that this sounded a lot like cognitive therapy, where puzzling or destructive behaviour is made comprehensible by bringing to light the premises and arguments that, if rehearsed in the mind of the individual involved, would logically lead them to act as they do.

'It is. It's very interesting. You can find out a lot about yourself by finding out which arguments you fudge. A lot of arguments are intrinsically difficult, so you would expect to make mistakes unless you had some training in logic. But a lot of familiar mistakes are ones people could not possibly make in neutral contexts. It's just that they are so convinced of the truth of their conclusions that they presume the supporting arguments must be right.'

We discussed a few recent dilemmas in bioethics that had caught the public imagination. One was the case of a couple who had lost their daughter. They were having another child through in vitro fertilization (IVF). It is perfectly possible in such a case to choose which of the fertilized ova is implanted in the womb by sex, and this is what the couple wanted to do. They wanted another daughter to, in some sense at least, replace the one they had lost. Many people found this abhorrent. How does Radcliffe Richards's method deal with the case?

The basic set up is simple: there is a presumption in favour of letting the parents have their choice. Can any good reason be found for preventing them?

'What we can't do is oppose it on the grounds that we shouldn't be interfering with nature. That won't do,' says Radcliffe Richards. This is in line with her general conviction that, post-Darwin, any appeal to the natural, or the need to avoid hubris, is hopeless.

'We seem to have a deeply ingrained idea of the dangers of interference in what is natural. It comes up in complaints about playing God, for instance. But you can only *interfere* with something which has a purpose or is meant to go a certain way. Darwinian nature as a whole isn't meant to go any way at all, it's just what happens. If it had gone another way, things might have been a great deal better – or worse. One of the phrases I was quite pleased about in the book is that however unreliable it is to try to make things go the way we want them to, it's infinitely more reliable than standing back and trying to let Darwinian nature take an Aristotelian course. If we want to achieve any good at all, standing back is not the way to do it.'

So arguments that appeal to talk about hubris or tampering with nature do not get off the ground as an objection to the couple who want to choose the sex of their baby. What does that leave?

'I can think of two possible reasons for saying that we should not allow this kind of choice. One is that allowing individual choice might seriously upset the balance of the sexes; we can already see trouble brewing in various parts of the world, where there are not enough women to go round. But that's probably not significant in this case. The couple do, after all, want a daughter. If sex ratios are seen as a potential problem, we could allow people to make reciprocal agreements with couples who wanted the other sex.'

The second reason is one Radcliffe Richards finds potentially more compelling. 'There can be good reasons for wanting to limit our own choices that have nothing to do with avoiding hubris. One such reason, for instance, is not having more responsibility than we can bear. Our species seems naturally prone to look for someone to blame when things go wrong; we blame parents for the way their children turn out as it is. Think how much more responsibility they would have to bear if they could make even more choices about their children. So that gives a kind of reason we might have for restricting reproductive choice – though actually I don't see that that is relevant to the couple who want to choose their child's sex. So my conclusion must so far be that there isn't an adequate reason for preventing the parents from choosing in this case.

'Cases like this are typical of ones where people's immediate responses are relics of earlier views of the world: ideas that there will be trouble if you interfere with the natural order. Of course lots of people do believe the world is divinely constructed, and has a moral order integrated with the natural order. But even among people who officially don't, these ideas show themselves in habits of thought. It requires real intellectual and logical work to see which of these intuitions have to be rejected, and work out what should be put in their place.

'One way of putting this is that there is a much greater distance between religious and secular ethics than is usually recognized, because moral thinking on both sides is so often blurred. I am a reluctant atheist – I'd much rather believe we lived in a world with an underlying moral order. But I don't think we do, and that any moral order is going to have to come from creatures like us; working seriously on post-Darwinian secular ethics is now my main concern.

'It's urgent, because the old habits do serious moral harm. For instance, look at all the fuss that's made about research on human embryos. Restrictions get in the way of research that might prevent significant suffering, while it is not at all clear that they achieve any good at all. And at the same time, this human-centred view of things allows us to take far less seriously the horrible cruelty we inflict on our fellow creatures. If the world is not as religions claim it is, there is real harm in acting as though it were.

'I'm afraid there's no escaping the underlying pessimism of a thoroughly secular view of ethics. Once you lose the idea that the universe is arranged to allow the eventual triumph of good, individual goodness becomes a tiny element of a morally indifferent whole, rather than a step towards eventual light. It makes me think of the old Norse idea that the forces of darkness would engulf everything in the end, but you should still be on the side of the gods and go down fighting. If good matters – as it certainly does – what else can you do? As they say, it is better to light a candle than to curse the darkness.'

Selected Bibliography

The Sceptical Feminist, 2nd edn (London: Penguin, 1994)
Human Nature after Darwin (London: Routledge, 2000)

3   Evolutionary Psychology

Helena Cronin

Evolutionary biological explanations of sexual behaviour and sex differences provoke strong reactions in their critics. For example, the recent publication of Thornhill and Palmer's *Why Men Rape* – in which they argued that all men are genetically capable of rape, given particular environmental or social stimuli – resulted in protests, calls for the cancellation of Thornhill's lecture programme, and Susan Brownmiller, author of the influential *Against Our Will: Men, Women and Rape* stating in the *Washington Post* that 'Thornhill gives sociobiology a bad name'.

In a similar vein, Hilary Rose, in *Red Pepper*, claimed that 'fundamentalist' Darwinists, 'with their talk of biological universals on matters of social difference are a political and cultural menace to feminists and others who care for justice and freedom' and that sociobiology 'has a history which varies from the dodgy to the disgusting on sexual difference'.

The target of Rose's attack was Helena Cronin, Co-director of the Centre for Philosophy of Natural and Social Science at the London School of Economics, and author of the highly acclaimed book *The Ant and the Peacock*. In a previous issue of *Red Pepper*, Cronin had begun an article on sex differences with this story. 'I recently heard a member of a girls' street gang boasting about their macho initiation ceremony. Recruits have to choose between being beaten up or having sex with a male gang member. Imagine making the same offer to male initiates. Sex not as a reward but as a penalty? Laughable.'

Cronin went on to show how the differences in sexual behaviour between men and women are rooted in biology. She concluded by noting that science tells us only what the world is like, and that our best bet if we want to change the world for the better is to let truth, rather than ignorance, be our guide.

Given the controversy, misplaced or not, that her arguments provoke, I ask Cronin what the key evolutionary facts are that make biological explanations of sex differences necessary.

'It stems from the fact that males and females have different reproductive strategies,' she answers. 'Think of it this way. Give a man fifty wives, and he can have children galore; but give a woman fifty husbands – no use at all. For men quantity pays, for women quality pays. In the evolution of our species, many men didn't breed at all whereas most women did; and some men vastly outbred others whereas women had about equal numbers of children. Thus, men's stakes – their potential gains, potential losses – were immensely higher than women's. So, generation after generation, down evolutionary time, natural selection favoured men with an appetite for multiple mates and a disposition to strive mightily for them. And, generation after generation, down evolutionary time, natural selection favoured women who chose prudently – for resources, protection, good genes.'

So the argument then is that males with a disposition to be competitive will do well, whereas males with a disposition to be prudent will do badly. And vice versa for females?

'That's right. We are all the descendants of victorious males and judicious females.'

The logic of the Darwinian approach is impressive, but what kind of empirical evidence is there to back up the claim that males and females display different patterns of behaviour and have different attitudes towards sex?

'Well,' replies Cronin, 'there's evidence from a multitude of independent sources. There are cross-cultural surveys; the largest study of mating patterns ever conducted, spanning 37 diverse cultures, bore out all the Darwinian predictions that were made – for example, everywhere women placing more importance on men's financial resources than men on women's; everywhere men caring more about women's looks than women about men's; everywhere women preferring husbands older than themselves and men preferring younger wives. And there are psychological experiments, ranging from how people answer questions to how they respond physiologically; so, for example, when asked to imagine their partner falling in love with or having sex with someone else, predictably the women were more jealous over loss of commitment, the men more over sexual infidelity – and this was reflected in physiological measures of stress. And then there are differences in sexual fantasies; lonely hearts columns; uses of pornography and prostitution; gay and lesbian sexuality. And this is just a small sample of the types of evidence.'

The point about men being more concerned than women about the possibility of their partner's sexual infidelity is interesting because it suggests that they might have developed sophisticated techniques in order to detect infidelity where it exists.

'Yes, men are indeed very sensitive to the possibility of infidelity. And it's something that women frequently don't understand,' responds Cronin. 'This aspect of men's psychology was designed to tackle a problem that women haven't had to face over evolutionary time. For a man, his partner's infidelity can involve not only losing her precious reproductive potential but even worse, in a species such as ours in which males invest heavily in their offspring, mistakenly investing in another male's reproductive success – a problem uniquely exacerbated in our species by concealed ovulation, which further lowers confidence of paternity. Males in all species that have faced similar problems have converged on similar solutions. Many male birds, for example, employ mate-guarding tactics – staying tenaciously close to the female while she is fertile; and experiments on some species have found that, if the male and female are separated during this period, the male's subsequent investment in the fledglings is reduced – the longer the separation the less the investment.

'In our species, one solution is male sexual jealousy. This encompasses a huge range of tactics, from vigilance – not letting the partner chat with other men at a party – to violence – sexual jealousy being the single most frequent cause of male domestic violence, from battering to murder. Another solution – in case those tactics fail – is to scrutinize the children for facial resemblance. The familiar question 'Doesn't it look like its dad?' comes routinely from the newborn's mother and her family; would-be fathers tend to suspend judgement. And men, but not women, prefer pictures of toddlers that resemble themselves, even though they are not conscious that this is the reason for their choice.'

The kind of Darwinian argument that Cronin is espousing goes further than the simple claim that males and females pursue different reproductive strategies. It is rather that these differences pervade their entire psychologies.

'Yes, that's right,' she says, when I ask her about this. 'Consider the case of men. Because they are built to play a higher-risk, higher-stakes game, they are far more competitive, risk-taking, opportunistic, persevering, single-minded, status-seeking, inclined to display, to show off. That is why men are more likely to die heroically, win a Nobel prize, drive too fast, commit murder. It is why they are overwhelmingly the stand-up comics, motor-bike riders, alcoholics, artists, child-abusers, mercenaries, pop stars, gamblers, sculptors, bungee jumpers, train spotters, computer nerds and CEOs. It is why such male excess is universal, transcending huge divides of nationality, culture, ethnicity, religion, politics, class and education; and why it manifests itself in modern societies across the globe and in every known record back through time.'

The major criticism of the kind of approach favoured by Cronin is that it ignores the impact of social factors in the construction of personalities and the moulding of behaviour. For example, in her *Red Pepper* article, Cronin cites a study of American college students, which showed that when asked by a stranger for a date, 50 per cent of both men and women agreed, but when asked 'Have sex with me tonight?', 75 per cent of men agreed compared to not one woman. But surely this difference is just as readily explained in terms of the social construction of gender, as it is in terms of natural selection, so why should we favour the Darwinian explanation?

'First,' responds Cronin, 'these sex differences can be predicted from fundamental Darwinian theory, from the difference between sperm – numerous, small, mobile, low unit-cost – and eggs – sparser, larger, rich with essential provisions. Sperm-bearers specialize more in competing for mates than in caring for offspring, and egg-bearers vice versa. In our species this sex difference is rather modest because men, too, are evolved to invest in offspring. But remember those 50 husbands versus 50 wives: men can get away with the briefest of encounters; women are committed to nine months hard labour, nutrient-rich milk, unceasing vigilance. These different investment portfolios cleave our species predictably into two.

'Second,' she continues, 'the same patterns can be found across all sexually reproducing species. From peacocks to stag beetles to elephant seals, males are more aggressive, more promiscuous, the show-offs and the risk-takers.

'Third, there's pathology. Nature's errors graphically demonstrate how hormones shape not only differing bodies but differing brains and thereby differing psychologies. If a female foetus is exposed to typically male hormones – androgens – in the womb, the child will be typically "tomboyish". And vice versa for males.

'Fourth, sex differences show up – universally – even in tiny children. At just a few days old girls are more interested in faces and making eye contact. At one year, girls stay closer to their mothers; boys wander off.

'Finally, sex differences are exceedingly robust across cultures, now and throughout history.'

Clearly, these are all reasons for favouring, at the very least, a Darwinian component in explanations of the differences in behaviour between the sexes. But they don't rule out alternative social explanations, so what is wrong with arguing that the *focus* should be on socialization rather than natural selection?

'To pit "socialization" or "learning" against evolved propensities is fundamentally misconceived,' answers Cronin. '"Socialization", or any other learning, is not an alternative to biology; it depends on biology. No individual, of any species, can learn anything without underlying adaptations for learning. Our innate capacities are what makes learning possible. Thus, socialization is successful only insofar as we are psychologically primed for it by natural selection. And, just as different species are appropriately differently primed, so too are males and females. Socialization is a biological issue.

'When applied to sex differences in particular, the "socialization" claim is that, left to their own devices, males and females would react identically to the same environments; and that the only reason why they systematically behave differently is that they are systematically exposed to different environments. This is comprehensively mistaken.

'There is scant evidence that parents, for example, do treat little boys and girls as claimed. Indeed, meta-analyses of studies in North America and Europe reveal that, if anything, parents discourage behaviour such as rough play and risk-taking more in young boys.

'But, more to the point, girls and boys, even new-born babies, react differently when exposed to the same environments – unsurprisingly, given the scrupulous care with which natural selection has shaped them differently, from bodies to brains.

'And, again, these sex differences occur in millions upon millions of other species, few of which even bring up their offspring at all, let alone teach them pink for girls and blue for boys.

'Finally, the cross-cultural robustness of sex differences starkly indicates that something other than purely arbitrary conditioning is afoot. Why don't sex differences occur in random directions? Why in, say, half the world's societies, don't parents care more about their sons' virginity than their daughters' or women prefer the lowest-status men? Why, indeed, aren't there societies with no sex differences at all?'

One possible response here is that the way in which socialization treats males and females is not arbitrary and, therefore, one should expect sex differences in behaviour to be robust across cultures. For example, there is the Engels-inspired argument that maintains that the sexual division of labour (i.e. males – workers; females – carers) is rooted historically in a need to guarantee clear lines of descent for the purposes of property inheritance, something that can only be achieved if women are confined to the domestic sphere. What is wrong with this kind of argument, I wonder?

'Well, there is a lot wrong with it,' Cronin insists. 'Consider first the specific Engels-style argument. A consistent conspiracy of all men against all women doesn't make Darwinian sense. Men do form coalitions against women; but they also have systematically conflicting interests, above all over mating. What's more, there was no property inheritance in the Pleistocene; but it was during this two-million year period that our sexual dimorphism evolved.

'But there are also more fundamental problems with all "socialization" theories of sex differences. One is that natural selection didn't build us to be putty in others' hands. Anyone who, in our evolutionary past, could be readily manipulated by all and sundry about anything, let alone about how to be successfully male or female, would never have become our ancestor. It's vanishingly unlikely that natural selection would leave it entirely to so-called "gender scripts" or "gender roles" to make boys into boys and girls into girls. After all, getting it wrong could spell reproductive oblivion.

'There's also the problem that, because these theories fail to spell out the psychological mechanisms on which "socialization" is assumed to rest, they get the causal pathways back-to-front. Certainly, boys are subjected to "macho" media images of males and girls to decorous images of females. But why assume that the media are creating macho or decorous behaviour? On the contrary, they are reflecting the evolved differences in boys' and girls' psychologies. One might as well argue that girls are socialized into growing breasts: after all, they aren't born with breasts; they develop them at the same time as their peer group; they are subjected to media images of girls with breasts; they grow up with a stereotype that all girls have breasts ...

'And, for the same reason, these theories are non-predictive. All that they can say is that whatever happens is socialization. But what would constitute a counterexample?

'By the way, there's an irony here. Those who champion socialization theories as a bulwark against what they envisage as "genetic determinism", have actually embraced what would be – if it were workable – rampant "environmental determinism". Children would be the puppets of adults, women the puppets of patriarchy, everyone the puppets of "media messages", advertising and linguistic spin ... indeed, any minds potentially the puppets of any others' manipulation.'

It is clear that Cronin believes that the case for a Darwinian explanation of sex differences is overwhelming. Why then, I ask, does she think that so many feminists and theorists on the Left are antipathetic to Darwinian theory?

'I think,' she answers, 'that the main reason is the notion that if something is biological then it can't be changed – and so political struggle is useless.'

But Cronin does not appear to share this concern, and rejects the charge of genetic determinism.

'Certainly, human nature is fixed,' she says. 'But the behaviour that it generates is richly varied. Our evolved minds are designed to enable us to react appropriately to the different environments in which we find ourselves. It is the variety, intricacy and sophistication of our innate mental machinery that makes possible the variety, intricacy and sophistication of our behaviour. So it is thanks to our genetic endowment, not in spite of it, that we are able to generate our impressive behavioural repertoire. The lesson for successful political engagement is clear. If you want to change the behaviour, then change the environment. But what constitutes a relevant environment and how we will react to it depends on our evolved minds. So an understanding of the evolved psychology of our species – of our dispositions and preferences, our motivations and desires – is vital for political action. That will tell us which aspects of our environment have to be altered in order to achieve the desired ends. The task, then, is to understand human nature, not to change it.'

It is striking that a theorist who considers herself a feminist is so vocal in championing the reality of biological differences between males and females. In this regard, I ask Cronin how her feminism stands in relation to the arguably still popular notion that women's sexual emancipation is best served by female sexuality becoming more like male sexuality.

'There are many ways in which women are held back and not allowed to realize their potential,' responds Cronin. 'Certainly, that applies to women's sexuality, which men world-wide, now and throughout history, have gone to great lengths to control, from veiling to harems, from genital mutilation to domestic violence. But the fashionable claim that females are just as promiscuous as males is wrong. This claim stems in part from a mistaken view that, in order to have fairness, you have to have sameness. But fair policies must be predicated on the way that the world really is; indeed, outcomes are likely to be less fair if predicated on mistaken assumptions.

'This fashionable view of female sexuality,' she continues, 'also stems from confusing the notion of promiscuity with the notion of enjoying sex. It is assumed that, because men are more inclined to be promiscuous, they enjoy sex more. But, on those grounds, one could equally well argue that the choosier you are, the more you are likely to enjoy sex – and so men enjoy sex less than women.

'And anyway,' concludes Cronin, 'why should women accept male values about the way that sexuality ought to be? Why on earth do would-be feminists adopt male standards of how to be sexual?'

It seems that the logic of Cronin's position is that what is possible for the future of female sexuality is quite clearly constrained by the way that natural selection has shaped men and women. I put this point to her.

'No,' she retorts, 'I wouldn't call that – or any other adaptation – a constraint. Natural selection shaped us to be able to speak a human language – do you call that a constraint? Natural selection shaped us to be able to fall in love – do you call that a constraint?'

But perhaps one might call it a constraint that natural selection has shaped us so that it is easiest to learn a language when we are relatively young. So isn't there a constraint with regard to female sexuality in that it is perhaps naïve for feminists to advocate as a political strategy equal levels of male and female promiscuity given the nature of their evolutionary development?

'I'd rephrase it,' responds Cronin, 'not equal levels – it is naïve for them to advocate *male* levels of promiscuity.'

There is a tendency among some philosophers to pour scorn on the work of evolutionary scientists. But it is clear from talking to Helena Cronin that there are both *a priori* and empirical reasons for taking their work very seriously indeed. Philosophers would do well to take note, or else they risk proving Edward O. Wilson right, that it is now science that most effectively addresses the great questions of existence and the meaning of the human condition.

Selected Bibliography

The Ant and the Peacock (Cambridge: Cambridge University Press, 1993)

4 Genes and Determinism

Richard Dawkins

There is a tendency among some philosophers to get worked up about a thing they call 'genetic determinism'. They seem to have in mind that a certain kind of neo-Darwinism reduces human beings to the status of automatons. If you ask them to specify which scientists they are thinking about, the most frequently mentioned names are probably Richard Dawkins and Edward O. Wilson. The belief seems to be that these writers think that human beings are destined only to follow blindly the dictates of their genes; that behaviour can be reduced to genes in such a way that exclusively genetic explanations of behaviour are full explanations.

The puzzle is that if you actually read the work of scientists like Dawkins and Wilson, it is obvious that they don't believe any such thing. But more than that, they explicitly state that they do not – Dawkins has described the idea of irrevocable biological determinism as 'pernicious rubbish on an almost astrological scale' – and in fact they explain in some detail why the idea just doesn't work. But despite this, the accusations of 'determinism', along with its counterpart 'reductionism', continue. It is these kinds of accusations, which seem to rely on a highly tendentious reading of the work of evolutionary biologists, which make an interview with Richard Dawkins both interesting and important. I begin by asking him about genetic determinism. He is on record as calling it a myth – what does he take the myth to be?

'I suppose the myth that there is something peculiar about genetic determinism as opposed to any other kind of determinism,' he replies. 'I recognize that philosophically speaking determinism is a difficult issue, which philosophers have been talking about for centuries. My point was that genetics has nothing to contribute to that philosophical argument. The argument will go on, and it is an interesting and important argument, but if you are a determinist you are a determinist, and adding the word genetic doesn't make it any more deterministic. There is nothing peculiar about genetic determinism which makes it particularly sinister.

'Also, when somebody announces that they have discovered a gene for let's say aggression or religion, this does not have a deterministic force in the sense of irrevocable determinism, any more than discovering that a particular chemical in a diet has an effect. You might find that people who eat red peppers are more aggressive than those who don't. I have no evidence for that, but you could find some such thing, and that's not deterministic either. That too will be a statistical effect that will be added in with all the other effects. Genes are to be thought of like that. They are statistical contributors to a complex, causal web – and that's all that matters for natural selection. The only reason that Darwinians talk about genes so much is that in order to do Darwinism they have to be looking at those aspects of individual variation in populations which are genetically influenced. So we're not talking determinism, we're talking statistics, we're talking analysis of variance, we're talking heritability.'

That this is how Dawkins sees the effect of genes is clear from reading his books. But one of the criticisms directed against him is that some of the language he employs can lead to misunderstanding. I ask him about one particular example, the idea of a 'gene for a particular behaviour'. What does it mean when evolutionary biologists use such terminology?

'This is a convention,' he answers. 'It means a gene such that if you change that gene to its allele, you might see a corresponding change in the phenotype. It is a contributor to phenotypic variance, it is a contributor to variation in a population. More specifically, when you compare the gene with its allele, you see a contribution to the variance.'

Phenotypes are normally understood to be the observable characteristics of organisms. They are determined by both genetic makeup and environmental influences. Examples of phenotypes include eye colour, tail-length and hair colour. Natural selection does its work on genes via the mechanism of phenotypes, because it is phenotypes that are visible to natural selection. Genes are differentially perpetuated to the extent that they give rise to phenotypes that enjoy selective advantages over other phenotypes, where the latter are also the product of genes, alternative genes, or *alleles*.

When Dawkins talks about genes for a particular behaviour, it seems then that he is not talking about causality in the sense that a gene determines *in toto* a phenotypic effect. He is rather talking about a web of causation.

'Yes,' agrees Dawkins, 'it is statistical causation. It is precisely the same sense of causation as when an agricultural scientist spreads nitrate in certain plots of a field and not other plots, and you do an analysis of variance of the size of wheat plants in these various plots, and you find that nitrate is a contributor to the variance. It is in that sense that nitrate does cause an increase in wheat size, but it is not the sole cause by any means, of course, and nor are genes. Genes exert their effects in exactly the same kinds of ways as the nitrate in this agricultural experiment.'

Perhaps the other sense in which the language in *The Selfish Gene* might have contributed to misunderstanding is in the use of the metaphor of *robots*. Indeed, Dawkins recognizes as much in *The Extended Phenotype*. But presumably he doesn't mean to suggest that robots are necessarily unthinking automatons?

'Far from it,' he replies. 'A robot to me, then and now, is potentially an exceedingly complicated and indeed intelligent being. I was using the word robot as almost a sort of poetic evocation of the idea that here is this fantastically complicated machine which has been programmed to do something. What interested me is that it has been in advance programmed to work by all manner of complicated, flexible and if necessary intelligent means towards one end, which is the propagation of the DNA which did the programming.'

There is arguably a certain irony in Dawkins's being accused of pure genetic determinism, because he is also famed for introducing the concept of *meme*. Memes are units of cultural inheritance – for example, a catchy tune – which are differentially successful in terms of their replication and survival. The irony is that memes, to the extent that they determine at all – and there is a sense in which you can be 'infected' by a meme (imagine a song that you cannot get out of your head) – are a kind of non-genetic determinism. I put this point to Dawkins and ask him whether he sees memes as being physiological entities (i.e. particular neural patterns in the brain), or as being pure code (i.e. the 'instructions' for building particular neural patterns in the brain).

'Well,' he replies, 'first, I should say that there is no irony, or certainly no contradiction at all in the concept of meme, because although it is non-genetic, it is a replicator. The point about introducing the concept of meme was not really to make a contribution to the study of human culture, but rather to say that Darwinism as a theory, in its most general form, is a theory of replicators, and DNA is just one kind of replicator. If you think in global, universal terms there could be other kinds of replicators. For example, if we travel to Mars there could be a completely different kind of life, different in all respects except that it will be based upon the differential survival of replicators of some other kinds, which might not be DNA, might not even be organic. Memes were originally introduced as a means of illustrating the principle that replicators do not have to be DNA.

'As to whether they are a useful concept to explain human culture, I'm not decided. It wasn't my original intention that they should be, but if they are, so much the better. There are people, really quite a lot of people, who use the meme concept as a proper constructive approach to understanding the human mind, among them Dan Dennett and Susan Blackmore, and also many lesser lights on the Internet.'

As to whether memes are physiological entities or pure code, Dawkins is undecided. 'I wasn't sufficiently clear and explicit about that originally. My colleague, Juan Delius, who is a neurophysiologist, in an article in the *Tinbergen Legacy* memorial volume, was much clearer, and actually stuck his neck out and said that a meme is a physiological entity which has phenotypic expression in the form of behaviour. But I think there are others who take an opposite view, who say that a meme is pure code, and it may reside in a printed page, or it may reside in a computer or a tape recorder, or in a brain.

'I'm happy to lay out these views as interesting alternatives, but I'm not quite sure which of these two views we should adopt. I suppose, almost thinking aloud now, you could say we should be looking for the memetic equivalent of the following statement about a gene: a gene is primarily thought of as a DNA sequence that resides in a cell and which has readout in the form of phenotype, but if a molecular biologist comes along and decodes the gene, and writes it out as a sequence of ATCG – the nucleotide bases of DNA – and prints it in a book, that book can then go on a library shelf and sit there for centuries. So I've translated the meme problem back into a gene problem, as is my wont, and you need to ask a biologist: is this stretch of ATCG, which occupies three and a half pages in a book, a gene, or is it the instructions for making a gene if you put it back into real physiology.'

An interesting facet of the meme idea is that it can be employed to explain why some people find Dawkins's work so hard to accept. It might simply be that the idea that we are survival machines for our selfish genes, although true, is not very attractive – perhaps because it is felt in some sense to diminish our humanity. I ask him whether he thinks that this might lie behind much of the knee-jerk reaction to his writing.

'Well, I'd rather not answer in meme terms,' he responds, 'but in more direct human terms – are people frightened of what I've said because they think it demeans our humanity? Yes, I think in some cases they probably are. I don't think that they've thought it through properly.'

His critics also appear not to have thought through properly the nature of an is/ought gap; that is, the logical impossibility of generating statements about how we ought to behave or how the world ought to be, from statements about facts. This is seen most clearly in their response to the way that Dawkins models sexual strategies, where some people seem to think, rather extraordinarily it must be said, that he is *advocating* a particular sexual strategy.

'It is absolutely extraordinary,' he agrees. 'It is the equivalent of saying that the natural state of humanity is to have no clothes, therefore we ought to go around with no clothes on. The most vocal and articulate culprit is probably Steven Rose, who actually used the very example you talk about, sexual strategies.

'I have in *The Selfish Gene* a very simple ESS – evolutionarily stable strategy – model of sexual strategies to make the point that a mixed strategy – somewhere between philanderer and faithful for males and coy and fast for females – is, under the conditions of the model, stable. Actually, it doesn't come out stable, it oscillates, which is a fascinating point, and which I didn't spot and nobody else spotted for quite a while. And that is genuinely interesting, the fact that it oscillates. What is not interesting is to treat it as a kind of political or ideological point and to suggest that I'm advocating philandering by human males. I mean it is not even as though the model ended up with philandering predominant, it actually ended up with faithful as the predominant strategy. And in fact with that model, humans weren't even mentioned. If anything I had a bird in mind. I'm not even very interested in humans to be honest.'

What, I wonder, motivates this kind of misunderstanding of his work? Is there a political or ideological agenda?

'Well, I don't know,' he replies. 'I think that some people just cannot conceive of anybody not being fundamentally interested in humans, so they assume that everything that you say must have human significance, and must have been intended to have human significance. They just cannot grasp that there are some interesting questions to be asked about evolutionary theory itself which may have very little connection with humans. Now that is disputable, some people think that it is very important for humans and some people don't, but I wasn't committing myself on that. I wasn't even very interested in it. I was interested in the theory itself, as it shows itself in computer models, as it might show itself in birds or in fleas. It's a fascinating theory to work out the consequences for. If it happens to work for humans so much the better, but that was not the primary interest.'

One of Dawkins's most striking claims – and indeed the central claim of *The Extended Phenotype* – is that genes make their presence felt not only in bodies, but also beyond bodies and across time and space.

'This, I suppose,' he tells me, 'is the main point of mine which is original. *The Selfish Gene* itself is just a vivid way of expressing orthodox neo-Darwinism, but the point about *action at a distance* or about genes having phenotypic effects outside the body is the contribution that *The Extended Phenotype* makes.

'Artefacts like caddis houses or birds' nests are Darwinian adaptations. Their shape, colour, hardness, size, every attribute about them that you could measure will turn out to be a Darwinian adaptation in very much the same way as a bird's eye or a lion's paw. It is incidental that the last two that I mentioned happen to be parts of a body, made of cells, and the other ones are not. The principle whereby Darwinian selection chooses genes on the basis of their phenotypic effects is identical in both cases. The phenotype that we define as a nest of a certain softness, colour, or curvature of lining has come about by Darwinian natural selection, and that has to mean natural selection of replicators and in this particular case genes. So genes proximally work by influencing embryonic development of the nervous system, or nest building behaviour, but the phenotypic consequences are the shape of the nest, the softness of the nest, the colour of the nest, and the logic of that is exactly the same as when you talk about the genes controlling the shape of a sheep's horn. It is all done by a complicated chain of embryological causation and it is incidental whether or not the chain of causation stops at the body wall or reaches out beyond the body wall and becomes something like an artefact outside the body.'

Part of the interest of arguments such as these is that they raise implications for issues to do with determinism, because they allow that the manipulation of one organism by another might be a function of the DNA of the manipulator. I ask Dawkins about this and specifically about the cuckoo.

'If you can do that logical trick for artefacts like caddis houses, you can also do it for other animals,' he explains. 'A cuckoo manipulates its host via the host's sense organs. A parasitic beetle that lives in an ants' nest secretes chemicals which mimic chemically the phero-mones that the ants use themselves, so the beetle can make the ants do things which are in the beetle's interest and not in the ants' own interest. Biologists have known about these kinds of manipulation for a very long time. But if you translate it into the language of the extended phenotype then it very simply falls out that the behaviour of the victim of the manipulation is a phenotypic effect of genes in the manipulator. And that is by the same logic as we say that the hairs on your toes are manipulated by genes in your own body.'

Related to this, there is a fascinating idea in the early chapters of *The Extended Phenotype* where Dawkins talks about an article that he wrote with John Krebs in which they described communication as a way in which one creature makes use of the muscle power of another. Is this a view that he still has sympathy with?

'Well, yes it is,' he replies. 'I support that view still. I suppose what has changed is that there are other ways of looking at communication which Krebs and I didn't talk about which are also helpful. But they are not incompatible with the manipulation view.'

I wonder whether there are any equivalents in humans. In fiction, we have Homer's *Sirens*, who lure sailors onto the rocks to their deaths by means of song.

'I think there are equivalents in humans,' he says. 'First, let's think about the relationship between humans and other species like horses. It is fascinating the way in which horses are "broken", which means that their will is broken. And they, though hugely more powerful animals, obediently turn left if you pull the left reign and right if you pull the right reign. And if you squeeze them with your heels they speed up, and so on. They do what they are told. They're not doing it because they want to or because they fear getting hit or not getting fed. There is a more direct manipulation that is achieved by exploiting the natural learning mechanisms of horses. So humans have worked out, consciously or unconsciously, how to manipulate horses by exploiting their natural learning mechanisms, so that the horse is being directly controlled by the human nervous system in a not dissimilar way to how its muscles are controlled by its own nervous system. It is just that humans control the horse's nervous system via its sense organs. Now relationships among humans might be characterized by a similar kind of manipulation.'

I suggest things like body-language and pheromones as likely examples of this kind of manipulation, and Dawkins agrees that they probably are. But he also mentions oratory. 'At the Nuremberg rallies, Hitler's voice, his choice of words, the sound of his voice, the general ambience of the huge crowds shouting *Sieg Heil*. I think that you can represent that as manipulation in much the same way as Krebs and I were talking about nightingales manipulating each other with their songs.'

The final question that I ask Professor Dawkins is about 'hard' determinism. At the end of *The Selfish Gene* he argues that humans alone on earth are able to 'rebel against the tyranny of the selfish replicators'. In other words, we alone are able to choose to act otherwise than perhaps our selfish genes would have it. However, for a hard determinist, the choices we make are themselves determined, they are the inevitable consequence of prior conditions, which at the moment of acting are set in concrete. In an interview in *The Third Way*, Dawkins indicated that he has some sympathy with Susan Blackmore's view that the self is just an illusion and that actually there are only brains and chemicals. I wonder then whether his position is that statements about consciousness or selfhood will ultimately be reducible to statements about neurons and chemicals?

'I suppose that philosophically I am committed to that view,' he admits, 'because I think that everything about life is a product of the evolutionary process and consciousness must be a manifestation of the evolutionary process, presumably via brains. So I think that has got to mean that consciousness is ultimately a material phenomenon. I mean that in the sense that there wasn't any consciousness before there was evolved life. Consciousness is not the kind of thing that was hovering around waiting for living things to embrace it. There wasn't anything remotely like consciousness before evolution had been going for the many millions of years it presumably takes to evolve the necessary nervous systems. Nervous systems may just be the way it works on our planet. I'm not saying that on Alpha Centauri there are not other kinds of consciousness that come from different sorts of mechanism. But they will come from mechanisms, and these I conjecture will be the product of an evolutionary process fundamentally similar to ours, and certainly similar in the sense that it will be by gradual evolution and not by any sudden leaping into action.'

This answer is significant because in claiming that consciousness is ultimately a material phenomenon it is clear that Dawkins is committed to a certain kind of reductionism, where reductionism is the explaining of one kind of thing in terms of other, in some sense more essential, kinds of things (as one might explain lightning, for instance, in terms of our knowledge about electricity). But this is not a surprise. He is on record as saying that reductionism is the most successful research stratagem ever devised. But, as he explained in the *New Scientist*, he is not interested in an unsophisticated reductionism, but rather one that emphasizes 'a multitude of highly sophisticated causal interactions, and mathematical relations'.

In one sense then, Dawkins's critics are right, ultimately his is a reductionist project, but crucially it is one that strips the term reductionist of any of its pejorative connotations. As to the other criticism that he embraces an irrevocable biological determinism, this interview makes it clear that this criticism is just wrong. Indeed, it is hard to imagine what else he can say to make this point any clearer.

Selected Bibliography

The Selfish Gene (Oxford: Oxford University Press, 1976)
The Extended Phenotype (Oxford: Oxford University Press, 1982)
The Blind Watchmaker (London: Penguin, 1986)

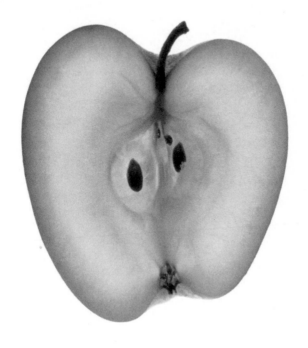

5 Science and Relativism

Alan Sokal

Before 1996, few philosophers had heard of Alan Sokal. A respected professor of physics at New York University, he was little known outside his profession. All that changed when he published a post-modern essay in the American cultural studies journal *Social Text*, 'Transgressing the boundaries: toward a transformative hermeneutics of quantum gravity'. It claimed, among other things, that 'a liberatory science cannot be complete without a profound revision of the canon of mathematics'.

The article got noticed because, once it was published, Sokal revealed that it was a hoax. The piece was a parody of what Sokal saw as the nonsense which often passed for serious scholarship in areas of the humanities and social science where post-modernism was popular. The article was followed by a fierce debate within academia and beyond, and then a book, *Intellectual Impostures* (written with Jean Bricmont), in which the spoof essay was reprinted along with a clear explanation of just what it was Sokal was objecting to: the misuse of science and a 'sloppy relativism'.

L'affaire Sokal, as it became known, was one of the intellectual events of the 1990s. For many it proved that the post-modern emperor had no clothes; for others, it showed how easy it was for critics to completely miss the point. But who exactly was this physicist who had caused such a rumpus?

When I met Sokal, I was reminded of the time when Dennis Healey compared a verbal attack by one of his parliamentary

colleagues to 'being savaged by a dead sheep'. Given the ferocity of
his intellectual assault, you might expect Sokal to be more lupine
than lamb-like. In fact, he is a friendly, chatty, slightly gauche figure
more interested in offering his guests his favourite blackcurrant tea
from New York than character assassinations. So how did this gentle
man come to be the scourge of the *rive gauche*?

'My original motivation had to do with epistemic relativism,'
explains Sokal. 'It seems to me that a sloppily thought-out relativism
has become the unexamined *Zeitgeist* in large sectors of the
American humanities and some parts of the social sciences. I also
had political motivations, because I was worried about the extent to
which that relativism was identified with certain parts of the
academic Left. I also consider myself on the Left, and I think
relativism is a suicidal attitude for the American Left.'

Sokal's intention was to write a parody of this kind of relativism
and to see if an academic journal would publish it. The end result
contained extensive quotations from the thinkers Sokal was
targeting, such as Jacques Lacan and Luce Irigaray, and pulled off
the powerful trick of constructing the parody almost entirely out of
the parodied (something which, ironically, some of the post-
modernists Sokal attacks would surely appreciate in another context).

'It's important not to exaggerate what the parody shows,' stresses
Sokal. 'As an experiment it doesn't prove very much. It just proves
that one journal was very sloppy in its standards. I don't know what
other journals would have done. I suspect that a lot of them would
have rejected it.

'As for the content of the parody, in some ways it's a lot worse
than a lot of stuff which is published, in some ways it's a lot less bad.
Steve Weinberg in his article in *The New York Review of Books* made, I
think, a perceptive observation – that, contrary to what some people
have said, the article isn't really incomprehensible. "The article
expresses views that I find surreal, but with a few exceptions Sokal at
least makes it pretty clear what these views are. ... I got the
impression that Sokal finds it difficult to write unclearly." Which is

absolutely true: I had to go through many revisions before the article reached the desired level of unclarity.

'It was a parody, intended to be extreme. In the first two paragraphs, it comes out and says, without any evidence or argument – of course it says it in high-faluting language, but translated into English it basically says – "Most Western intellectuals used to believe that there exists a real world, but now we know better."'

By the time the parody had been published and Sokal had revealed the hoax, provoking a storm that became big news in the quality press in France, Britain and America, the original target had been extended.

'As I did the research for the parody I came up against another issue, namely, the gross abuse of terminology from the natural sciences in the writings of French, American and British academics. The French ones are the more prominent, they're the big stars. The Americans who write nonsense about chaos theory or quantum mechanics are in general much less well known.'

The parody was thus to spawn a book, *Intellectual Impostures*, published in France in 1997 and in English in 1998, covering both relativism and the abuses of science. 'It was the second aspect that became the most sensational aspect of the book, but it was the question of relativism that motivated me.'

However, the coverage of the two themes in one book has perhaps back-fired, in that readers have confused the two issues.

'One thing that I have to emphasize over and over and over again, and which we emphasize in the preface to the English edition, but somehow it doesn't seem to sink in, is that there are really two books under one cover, which are only weakly related. There is the critique of the gross abuses of scientific concepts by certain French philosophico-literary intellectuals (they're not all philosophers in the strict sense). Then, on the other hand, there are various versions of epistemic relativism which we criticize; here the targets are mainly British and American, not French, and the two debates are on very different planes. They have to be evaluated completely separately, the targets are different. We do not accuse the authors of the impostures of relativism. In some cases it's not clear what their philosophy is, and we don't make any attempt to judge it. Conversely, concerning the authors of relativism, we don't accuse them of imposture; we accuse them of ambiguous writing or sloppy thinking, but certainly not of trying to misrepresent things. So the two discussions are completely separate, and the link between them is primarily sociological.'

Sokal's frustration that people don't notice this separation, when it is so clearly stated in the preface, tells you all you need to know about what motivates him: he just can't stand it when people fail to notice clear, logical distinctions, and having to repeat them until people do get it just irritates him more. Critics have claimed that this scientific insistence on clear, neat distinctions just isn't relevant to the texts he lampoons. Sokal is not impressed by the objection, voiced most explicitly by John Sturrock in the *London Review of Books*. 'Sokal and Bricmont,' wrote Sturrock, 'apply criteria of rigour and univocity fundamental to their own practice [as physicists] which are beside the point once transferred to this alien context.'

'What criteria of rigour are we talking about?' asks a frankly baffled Sokal. 'Are we talking about the idea that a sentence should mean something relatively determinate; that the words in it should mean something arid have some relevance to the subject at hand; that there ought to be a logical argument from one sentence to another; that when you're talking about some external phenomena, the facts about those phenomena are relevant? I mean, we're upholding the minimal standards of evidence and logic that I would have thought would be taken for granted by anybody in any field.'

What of the idea that there's a certain value to be had simply in a kind of liberal attitude to ideas? Sturrock goes on to say, 'far better wild and contentious theses of this sort [Irigaray's] than the stultifying rigour so inappropriately demanded by Sokal and Bricmont'.

Sokal's retort is sharp: 'But he doesn't say what is so stultifying

about the notion that the sentences should mean something and that there should be some logical connection between them. If he thinks it is important for crazy ideas to be out there and not suppressed, then fair enough. The question is, "should they be out there and criticized, or out there and uncriticized?" He seems to be saying that they should be out there and uncriticized, that it's unfair to point out that these wild and contentious theses are in fact crazy.'

Sokal's argument seems pretty irresistible. But what if we take an extreme defence and say that vagueness and ambiguity are actually great virtues in writing because they open up possibilities, which, again, Sturrock suggests?

'Well in poetry it's a great virtue, in novels it might be a great virtue. But I do think that in analytical writing, whether it's about physics or biology or history or sociology, the goal should be to remove ambiguity when possible. Of course, natural language is unavoidably ambiguous, but we should do our best. If we're trying to talk about some external objects, then we should try to make as clear as possible which external objects we're talking about and what we're saying about them.

'When the book came out in France, Jean-François Lyotard agreed to be on a television programme with Bricmont and me, and we had a kind of debate. Unfortunately it wasn't a very serious programme (their usual fare was sex scandals). Alas, the fifteen-minute debate consisted of a ten-minute monologue by Lyotard in very flowery French, in which, if I understood him correctly, he was saying that you physicists don't understand that words are used in a different way in poetry and novels than they are in physics books. When we finally got the floor, we said, yes, we know that, but to our knowledge the books of Lacan and Deleuze are not sold in the poetry section of bookstores – they are sold in psychology and philosophy, so they should be judged by the standards of psychology and philosophy. Those are cognitive discourses, they are purporting to say something about something, let's judge them that way. If you want to reclassify them as poetry, then we can judge them on whether they're good poetry or not. My personal feeling would be most of these people don't write good poetry either, but that's another story.'

However, when reading Sokal and Bricmont's book it can feel as though one is just being invited to laugh at all these foolish people. The principle of charity implores us always to seek out the most plausible interpretations of a piece of writing. Did Sokal flout this principle?

'Let's not leave this as an abstract question in the air,' insists Sokal. 'This is an open challenge to the defenders of all the authors we criticize. We would love for people to pick one or more passages in the book where we criticize particular texts and explain first of all what they mean, then justify the references to mathematics and physics and explain why the argument is valid. So far, no one has taken up our challenge. There was one article in *La Recherche* where two Lacanians tried, rather vainly I thought, to defend Lacan's dentification of the square-root of minus-one with the erectile organ. But aside from that, our critics have offered only abstract defences of the right to metaphor – something we grant, explicitly, in our very first chapter – but without trying to defend any specific one of the texts we criticize.'

Sokal tries to maintain a tricky equilibrium between his strongly held views about relativism and his avowed lack of interest in getting drawn into subtler philosophical debates. Whether this is tenable is unclear. Very few people are crude relativists, as Sokal acknowledges. So then doesn't he have to get involved in the subtler philosophical issues if he wants his case to stick?

This perhaps came out in a lengthy exchange I had with Sokal about the differences between idealism, relativism and instrumentalism. Idealists believe that there is no such thing as a mind-independent reality, but it doesn't follow from this that science is not objective. Relativists believe that there is no one truth about reality. Instrumentalists believe that science is not about discovering the nature of reality, but a means of predicting and manipulating the world. These positions can all be classified as non-realist, in that they either deny the existence of a world independent of minds, or else at least deny that such a world can be known. Sokal, who sees himself as a moderate realist, is strongly opposed to relativism and less stridently opposed to instrumentalism. But if a broad idealism is behind a lot of the thinkers he criticizes, and that is distinct from instrumentalism and relativism, then he's not only missed his target, he's also not really in the right ball-park.

Whether or not this is the case is a moot point, but when I spoke to him, Sokal seemed to be able to make sense of idealism only in terms of either instrumentalism or relativism. At one point, Sokal said, 'But I haven't figured out what this idealist is saying. Is the idealist saying that there does or does not exist a world outside my mind?' The answer, I suggest, is that 'the world exists outside your mind but not outside all minds.' 'I don't understand,' replied Sokal.

I say this not to expose the limits of Sokal's philosophical knowledge (he is well aware of them himself and it's abundantly clear that Sokal is much clearer in his understanding of philosophy than his targets are about the science they appropriate), nor because I am sure that idealism is behind a lot of what Sokal criticizes, but rather to illustrate the perils of Sokal's enterprise. He wants to avoid the subtle distinctions and stick to the gross errors. But is it not possible that some of these only appear as gross errors because of a lack of understanding of the subtler ideas underlying them?

Sokal insists that, 'the debate I was trying to raise was much cruder. We give the example of the anthropologist who was discussing two theories of the origin of native American populations: one, that they came from Asia, which is the archaeological consensus; the other, the traditional Native American creation myths, according to which their ancestors always lived in the Americas. And the anthropologist said, "science is just one of many ways of knowing the world. The Zunis' world-view is just as valid as the archaeological viewpoint of what prehistory is about." So, in the book we go through and try to disentangle the various things he could mean by "just as valid". There are certain interpretations of that which are unobjectionable but don't say much, there are other versions that do say something significant but which we think are grossly false. Jean [Bricmont] and I were in Brazil in April for a two-day seminar at the University of São Paolo about our book and related topics, and we had long discussions with anthropologists who refused to admit that a culture's cosmology could be objectively true or false. Their beliefs about the origin of the universe or the movements of the planets could only be judged true or false relative to a culture. And not just questions of cosmology, also questions of history. So we asked, "Is the assertion that millions of native Americans died in the wake of the European invasion not an objective fact of human history, but merely a belief that's held to be true in some cultures?" We never got a straightforward answer from them.'

Whether or not Sokal is right in his accusations, his methods, particularly the parody, have been criticized on some fronts for undermining certain important things, such as trust. Does perhaps the ridiculing of an area of academia bring the whole intellectual community into disrepute? 'There's certainly a danger. I have to emphasize that I didn't expect that this would ever reach the man on the street. It certainly wasn't intended to reach the front page of *The New York Times* or the front page of the *Observer* or the front page of *Le Monde*. A month before it came out in *Social Text*, I was discussing with my friends, "how big is this likely to be?" My prediction was that it would be a significant scandal within a small academic community. It would be page ten of the *Chronicle of Higher Education* [the American equivalent of *The Times Higher*] and maybe a 50:50 chance of a brief mention on *The New York Times* education page. So I certainly didn't expect that it would make the popular press and, indeed, when it did, some of the articles in the popular press, even in the so-called serious press like *The New York Times*, gave off a whiff of anti-intellectualism, which I've tried to criticize in my writings since then.

'Yes, in the popular press it had briefly two negative effects. It was used to bash intellectuals in general and it was used to bash the political Left in general. At every opportunity I've had I've argued

against both of those two misuses. It's not an attack on intellectuals in general. It's a critique by some intellectuals of other intellectuals. And it's not an attack of the Left in general, it's a critique by someone on the Left against others on the Left.' As a physicist criticizing people in humanities, I wonder if Sokal has ever felt like an impostor.

'No. I've felt lots of times that perhaps I'm getting in over my head, which is a totally different thing. We emphasize in the introduction to our book that everybody has the right to express their ideas about anything, whatever their professional credentials are, and the value of the intervention has to be determined by its contents, not by the presence or absence of professional credentials. So physicists can say perfectly stupid things about physics or the philosophy of physics, and non-physicists can say perfectly smart things about physics, it depends upon what's being said. So, of course, sometimes I'm a little scared because I know I'm venturing outside of the area of my primary competence. A lot of the book is on our area of primary competence, namely mathematics and physics, but one chapter is on philosophy of science, which is a little bit out of our area. So of course I'm a little worried that perhaps I've made some stupid mistake and the philosophers are going to take us to task for it.'

L'affaire Sokal was brief, and after it was over Sokal returned to his 'first love', mathematical physics. How did the affair alter his perceptions of the humanities and social sciences?

'The best thing about this whole affair for me, which has now taken about three years of my life, has been that I've been able to meet and sometimes become good friends with really interesting people in history, philosophy and sociology that I wouldn't have otherwise met. From them I've found out both that things were worse than I thought, in the sense that some of the sloppy thinking was more widespread than I had imagined, and also that things were better than I thought, in that there were a lot of people within the humanities and social sciences who had been arguing against sloppy thinking for years and often were not being heard. After the parody and again after the book I got an incredible amount of emails from

people in the humanities and social sciences and people on the
political Left as well, who were saying, "thank you, we've been trying
to say this for years without getting through, and maybe it was
necessary for an outsider to come in and shake up our field and say
that our local emperor is running naked".'

Selected Bibliography

Intellectual Impostures, with Jean Bricmont (London: Profile Books, 1998; 2nd
    edn, 1999)

6 Science as the New Philosophy

Edward O. Wilson

In the late 1970s, Edward O. Wilson, Professor of Science and Curator of Entomology at the Museum of Comparative Zoology, Harvard, was probably the most controversial scientist in the world. The cause of his notoriety was the book, *Sociobiology: The New Synthesis*, in which he argued – mainly in the final chapter – that certain kinds of human social behaviour can be understood in genetic terms. The response to its publication was furious: the American Anthropological Association debated a motion to censure sociobiology; a group of Boston scientists – including Steven Jay Gould and Richard Lewontin, both colleagues of Wilson at the Museum of Comparative Zoology – formed 'The Sociobiology Study Group', noting in *The New York Review of Books* that theories that attempted to establish a biological foundation to social behaviour provided an 'important basis ... for the eugenic policies which led to the establishment of gas chambers in Nazi Germany'; and Wilson himself was drenched with water by protestors at a meeting of the American Association for the Advancement of Science in early 1978.

Twenty-five years on, and things are different. We are now used to thinking about human behaviour in genetic terms, and much of the heat has gone out of the sociobiology debate. Indeed, Wilson himself, in a recent *Guardian* interview, declared that he thinks that the sociobiology controversy is essentially over. 'The contrarians are ageing,' he told Ed Douglas. 'No young scientists are joining. They are not handing on the torch but passing it around a smaller and dwindling circle.'

Wilson's good reputation is assured. He has won numerous awards, including the USA's National Medal of Science and the Pulitzer Prize twice. In 1995, *Time* magazine named him as one of the 25 most influential people in America. And his colleagues speak glowingly of him. Bryan Appleyard, for example, proclaimed Wilson to be 'the most important scientist of the late twentieth century'. Richard Dawkins has described him as an 'outstanding synthesizer'. And Jared M. Diamond, writing in *The New York Review of Books,* rated Wilson 'among the leading biologists and scientific thinkers of this century'.

However, while it is true that sociobiology no longer provokes the extreme reactions that it once did, many of the issues that lay behind the controversy are still alive today. Perhaps most significant is the issue of 'reductionism' and its suitability as a strategy for explaining human behaviour and cultural phenomena. In the eyes of the critics of reductionism, such a strategy results in the claim that complex behaviours are straightforwardly genetically determined. For example, Steven Rose, Leon Kamin and Richard Lewontin assert in *Not in Our Genes* that 'sociobiology is a reductionist, biological determinist explanation of human existence. Its adherents claim ... that the details of present and past social arrangements are the inevitable manifestations of the specific actions of genes.'

However, Rose *et al.* are not in any straightforward sense correct. Even a cursory reading of the work of serious sociobiologists reveals that they do not argue for inevitable genetic determinism. For example, Richard Dawkins devotes a chapter of his book *The Extended Phenotype* to debunking what he calls the 'myth of genetic determinism'. And in his 1998 book, *Consilience*, Wilson notes that 'all biologists speak of the interaction between heredity and environment. They do not, except in laboratory shorthand, speak of a gene "causing" a particular behaviour, and they never mean it literally.'

However, while Wilson rejects the accusation of genetic determinism, he is happy to embrace reductionism. In *Consilience*, he describes it as the primary and essential activity of science: 'It is the search strategy employed to find points of entry into otherwise impenetrably complex systems. Complexity is what interests scientists in the end, not simplicity. Reductionism is the way to understand it.'

Indeed, the central thesis of *Consilience* is that everything in our world is potentially analysable in terms of a small number of irreducible laws and, therefore, that a fundamental unity of knowledge is a reasonable and realizable goal. The book is a *cri de coeur* for the resurrection of Condorcet's Enlightenment vision, which held that human progress is inevitable and without definite limits. However, Wilson recognizes that, as yet, consilience is a hypothesis, albeit a plausible one: 'Universal consilience,' he tells me, 'cannot be proved by logic based on irrevocable assumptions now available. The assumptions behind universal consilience appear to grow sounder all the time, the more we learn about human biology, the mind, and culture, but they are not yet beyond all reasonable doubt.'

Nevertheless, despite the provisional nature of his thesis, he recognizes that it will raise the hackles of many professional philosophers. 'The subject I address they consider their own,' he writes, 'to be expressed in their language, their framework of formal thought. They will draw this indictment: conflation, simplism, ontological reductionism, scientism and other sins made official by the hissing suffix. To which I plead guilty, guilty, guilty.' What, I ask him, does he suspect to be at the root of their suspicion?

'It appears to me,' he replies, 'that professional philosophers have not kept up with the foundational disciplines of neuroscience, behavioural genetics, and evolutionary biology, and as a result have surrendered their franchise to the scientists. The scientists, not the philosophers, now address most effectively the great questions of existence, the mind, and the meaning of the human condition. This surrender seems to be permanent, and professional philosophers have begun a diaspora into other vital and challenging disciplines that include theoretical neuroscience, evolutionary theory, intellectual history and bioethics.'

However, I wonder whether there is more to their suspicion than simply a kind of professional jealousy. Is it not that some philosophers just doubt the usefulness of reductionist explanations? For example, John Searle has argued that a causal explanation of the functioning of a car engine is always likely to be superior when couched at the level of cylinder blocks and pistons rather than at the quantum level of quarks and muons, because it will never be possible to understand the functioning of an engine at the quantum level. Is this a view that Wilson has any sympathy with?

'No,' he insists, 'the way you've stated it is a misunderstanding of science. Major science always deals with reduction *and* resynthesis of complex systems, across two or three levels of complexity at a step. For example, from quantum physics to the principles of atomic physics, thence reagent chemistry, macromolecular chemistry, molecular biology, and so on – comprising, in general, complexity to reduction, and reduction to resynthesis of complexity, in repeated sweeps.'

This is both a plausible defence of reductionism and also a clear statement of what is involved in the consilient project. It is striking that Wilson is so upbeat about this project, because the idea that it is possible to uncover what might be called the absolute truth about nature and its workings, describable in terms of unified laws of physics, runs counter to virtually all post-modernist thinking, which stresses the linguistic, social and historical context of knowledge. How then have the post-modernists got it so wrong and why should we be optimistic that we'll develop forms of knowledge that transcend our limitations as evolved biological organisms?

'Post-modernist thinkers ignore the evidence for general principles that link particularity of experience,' Wilson replies. 'They may describe brilliantly the immediate neighbourhood in which they exist, but without a map they have no idea where they are or how to get from one place to another. I'm optimistic because the map available, mostly through the natural sciences, is getting better all the time, and is filling the gaps between brain and mind, and mind and culture, swiftly. Why not stress linguistic, social and historical contexts *and* the consilient principles that link them?'

Despite his optimism, however, Wilson does recognize that the consilient project faces considerable barriers. Perhaps the greatest, I suggest to him, is the difficulty of explaining consciousness or the mind in exclusively physical terms, something that many people believe is ruled out by its first person nature. The 'hard problem' of consciousness, as it has been termed by David Chalmers, is to explain why things like pain *feel* like anything at all. I ask Wilson what kind of conceptual apparatus he envisages as necessary to leap the explanatory gap between descriptions of physical processes in the brain and an understanding of the subjective nature of conscious experience.

'The empirical mapping of symbolic representation, scenario formation (with the self included) and emotion-mediated scenario competition,' he replies. 'We have a long way to go, but when these processes are depicted accurately enough, I believe we will have a generally acceptable explanation of consciousness. As to Chalmers's hard problem, I never thought it hard, as I explained in *Consilience*.'

This response, though straightforward and to the point, raises lots of questions. Particularly, many philosophers – though by no means all – will be discomfited by such a summary dismissal of the hard problem of consciousness. The root of the hard problem is as follows. It is possible that science might explain the performance of all the cognitive and behavioural functions that accompany experience, and yet there remains a further unanswered question: *why* is the performance of these functions accompanied by experience at all? According to Chalmers, in *The Conscious Mind*, 'this further question is the key question in the problem of consciousness. Why doesn't all this information-processing go on "in the dark", free of any inner feel?' Wilson's response in *Consilience* is to show how science might 'illuminate subjective experience' by developing mechanisms that will allow us access to each other's mental states. However, it is at least arguable that this response does not fully address the hard problem, which is not about developing a genuine intersubjectivity of experience, but rather explaining why there is subjective experience at all.

A similar tension accompanies Wilson's treatment of the other area where people might most doubt the utility of a consilient approach, namely, in the field of ethics. Much of the doubt will reside in the seemingly logical impossibility of generating statements about how we *ought* to behave from the kinds of statement of fact that are the province of science. This is what is known as the 'is/ought' gap. But Wilson doesn't appear to accept the force of this argument, writing that 'to translate is into ought makes sense if we attend to the objective meaning of ethical precepts'. So I ask him what he takes to be the 'objective meaning of ethical precepts' and how they function to translate 'is' into 'ought'.

'The objective meaning of ethical precepts comprises the mental processes that assemble them,' he responds, 'and the genetic and cultural histories by which they evolved. Those who think that an is/ought gap exists have not reasoned through the way the gap is filled by mental process and history. Eventually, and the sooner the better, we'll be able to base moral reasoning on this kind of objective idea of meaning, creating as it does a firmer understanding of the consequences of choices made among ethical precepts.'

The idea here seems to be that ethical precepts – for example, the incest taboo – have their roots in particular and explicable genetic and cultural histories. It is clear that understanding such histories will be a useful tool in making ethical judgements. What is less clear is that this is a way out of the is/ought problem. After all, I ask, are there not circumstances in which we will do well to struggle to behave in ways that might seem contrary to our natural instincts, as, for example, with respect to ethical precepts rooted in a mistrust of strangers or in aggression responses?

'Yes,' Wilson agrees, 'that's why we have to replace the is/ought shorthand with analysis of the objective meaning of ethical precepts. We no longer live in the Palaeolithic environment in which our still-existing instincts were favoured by natural selection.'

The idea that it is possible to bring to bear the tools of science to the field of ethics will not only lead to raised eyebrows because of the problems that are believed to be inherent in the is/ought gap, but also because it will be seen to be an example of the way in which science encroaches on domains that have previously been dominated by other kinds of rationality. The general fear here is that science is becoming an authoritarian monolith, one that precludes other kinds of thoughts and insights. Related to this is the fear that the kinds of ideas espoused in *Consilience* are part of a process that will inevitably lead to the general feeling that human existence is cold and meaningless. Are these, I wonder, worries that Wilson recognizes?

'Sure, I recognize the problem,' he admits, 'but even with the gathering of universal consilience, if it is proven correct, we are still entering a vast domain of the unknown. I'd rather go there with more rather than less confirmable knowledge and a lot less superstition. And, human nature being – genetically – what it is, we'll be challenging, quarrelling, and innovating every step of the way.'

But why, I ask, should we be confident that the consilient world-view will ever be espoused by more than perhaps a few scientists and philosophers? After all, by Wilson's own reckoning we haven't evolved to interpret and react to the world in this kind of measured way. And other world-views are arguably more attractive in their ability to answer existential questions.

'I agree that it is a tough sell,' he responds, 'because in the attractiveness of religious and ideological dogma, we evolved by natural selection, to accept one kind of truth, but with science and technology we have discovered another. Eventually, because science is by definition provable and entirely democratic – that is, dismissive of the boundaries between people – it seems likely that a consilient world-view will win out.'

It is interesting that despite the fact that the pre-eminence of the consilient world-view is not assured, Wilson seems to be much more relaxed than scientists such as Richard Dawkins about the prospect that religion will remain part of the dominant culture for the foreseeable future. What explains this relaxed attitude?

'I think religious belief, and the transcendentalist world-view, will prevail among most people for generations to come, even as the global techno-scientific civilization they depend upon determines most of their day-to-day thinking and activity. At the same time, traditional religions will moderate by becoming increasingly secularized: their believers cannot afford to depart too far from the evolving global culture. Fundamentalism, recent studies have shown, is a product more of internal dissension than of the triumph of dogma. So for scientists and others who worry about the grip of religious faith, I say continue to light a brighter candle and chase back the darkness.'

Selected Bibliography

Sociobiology: The New Synthesis (Cambridge, MA: Harvard University Press, 1978)
Consilience (London: Little, Brown and Co., 1998)

7 Science and Religion

Russell Stannard

In his book, *The God Experiment*, the physicist Russell Stannard talks about a 'prayer experiment' that is currently under way in the United States. The participants are 1,200 heart surgery patients. Half of these will be prayed for by a group of volunteers, the other half will not be. The patients themselves, while knowing that they are part of an experiment, will not know whether they have been prayed for or not. The point of the experiment is to find out whether after two years there are significant differences in the progress of the two groups. In other words, the experiment is designed to test the efficacy of prayer and thereby perhaps tell us something about the existence of God.

Stannard's book, *The God Experiment*, is a widening out of the prayer experiment. It is an attempt to look at a whole range of evidence, most particularly that offered up by science, in order to determine whether the hypothesis of God's existence is supported. This endeavour is quite unusual because many scientists and theologians insist that science and religion deal with different kinds of questions. Stannard tells me that this is a view with which he has some sympathy.

'Very broadly speaking, science is concerned with "how" questions, whereas religion is more concerned with "why" type questions, why are we here, what's the purpose of life and that sort of thing. Science is successful because it delineates the kinds of questions that it can answer. As long as it sticks to its brief, it's unsurpassed.

'But,' he continues, 'I don't believe that science and religion are hermetically sealed from each other, there are points of contact between the two. For example, there has always been this religious idea that human beings are basically flawed; that we are self-centred rather than God-centred. And therefore that it requires a positive act to repent, to reorient yourself to become God-centred. This idea underpins much of Christian theology.

'However, until fairly recently one had to accept this notion of "original sin" on trust. But as soon as you come to evolution by natural selection, and you realize that there are in-born tendencies encoded in the DNA, and that they're all to do with survival, then that leads to the question what kinds of in-born tendencies are there in human beings as evolved animals. And certainly, selfishness is one of them. Therefore, you would expect from the moment of conception that there is this tendency to be selfish, which has got to be combated if you're going to make your life God-centred. So, in this example, science confirms a part of Christian theology, and in that sense science and religion are not hermetically sealed from each other.'

While there can be no doubt that science has an impact on theology, not least in the sense that modern theologians modify their beliefs in light of scientific discoveries, it is not so clear that it works the other way around. Presumably Stannard does not think that science in any way requires religion?

'Science is not dependent on religion,' he agrees. 'You can be a thoroughly good, prominent scientist, without being religious. And science itself can indeed proceed in a watertight way, with the sort of questions that it deals with – the "how" questions. But as soon as you start saying, where did this world come from, why is there anything at all, science says, well those aren't scientific questions, I'm not going to answer them.'

I wonder whether Stannard thinks that this is a fair response. Are these in fact the kinds of questions that science should just leave alone?

'Well, I think they are perfectly good questions,' he replies. 'If nothing exists, then that seems to me to be a state that does not call for explanation. It seems quite natural that nothing should exist. But as soon as something exists, then you have problems. Why does it exist? Why is it this universe, rather than some other? Why is it an intelligible universe? Why is it run by laws? Why these laws, rather than some other set of laws? It seems to me that as soon as something exists then it calls for an explanation, whereas a state of nothing does not require explanation.'

But does this mean that he also thinks that God's existence requires some kind of explanation?

'Well, one way of approaching theology is to *define* God as the source of all existence,' he answers. 'In other words, given that you have existence, it seems a perfectly natural question to ask what is the explanation for existence, and the answer is – whatever is the ground of all being, and that is what I call God.'

There is a problem with this reply, and it is one identified by the evolutionary biologist Richard Dawkins. It seems strange to argue that the universe must have an explanation, and that it must be sustained in some way by a creator, and yet simultaneously to maintain that this creator, presumably an extremely intelligent and complex being, itself does not require explanation. I put this point to Stannard.

'Well,' he responds, 'there is a category mistake going on here. God is not just one more existent thing, which is then the cause of the universe, because if that was the case then you are in the Dawkins type problem.'

But it is not clear that this reply avoids the difficulty. The category mistake only occurs because God is defined in a certain way. It seems then that the problem is ruled out simply on definitional grounds. But significantly, the same move can be made when considering the existence of the universe; that is, the universe can be defined as the kind of entity, the existence of which does not need explanation.

'Yes,' admits Stannard, 'that is the line that Dawkins would take.

He obviously feels comfortable with it, but I don't, because of all the particularities of this universe. I just instinctively feel that as soon as the world exists, questions arise – why this world, rather than some other world? One of my concerns about this kind of argument, or other arguments about science and religion, is that many people get involved in them on the understanding that it is possible to be argued into a belief in God. I don't think that anybody has ever been argued into a belief in God.'

This is an interesting response, because it seems that Stannard is conceding that arguments about scientific evidence are never going to be enough to persuade someone that God exists. That being the case, I wonder whether anything was up for grabs in the writing of *The God Experiment*. Is it possible that he might have reached different conclusions, or does personal experience – in his case, the experience of a loving God – trump everything?

'Well,' he answers, 'in *The God Experiment*, I am really saying that the whole of life is a kind of experiment, where different kinds of questions and indications of God crop up, the most important one being one's own prayer life. It is possible to argue as much as you like about the source of existence, or about the anthropic principle, but if that was all that I had to go on, I would not believe in God. Or it would be a belief that did not affect me. By far and away the most important aspect of religious life is one's own personal dealings with God.'

I wonder whether this means that it is quite reasonable for someone who does not have a personal relationship with God to conclude, on the basis of the evidence that Stannard considers in his book, that there is no justifiable reason for a belief in God?

'I would simply say,' Stannard answers, 'that they have not done the most important part of the experiment, which is to give prayer a genuine try.'

This is all very well, but it seems that in privileging prayer like this, Stannard has moved well away from the kinds of procedures that would normally be considered scientific, particularly in that prayer takes place in a hidden domain.

'Yes,' admits Stannard, 'it does take you out of the public domain, where you can say here is an experiment, you're looking at it, I'm looking at it, and we can agree on the evidence. This is crucial for the physical sciences, but I have never made the claim that theology is like the physical sciences. However, if you're thinking in terms of say psychology, and both Freud and Jung regarded psychology as a science ...'

I interrupt here, because psychologists have precisely the same concern about the scientific validity of introspective reports. Indeed, the whole behaviourist movement in psychology can be seen as a response to just these concerns, where they attempted to put into a 'black box' the kind of introspective evidence that had dominated psychology up to that point.

'Okay, let's take physics as an example,' he responds. 'I believe a lot of things about physics, not having personally done the experiments. And it is because I trust the people who have done the experiments. It seems to me that if you're dealing with religious people, who all engage in this prayer activity, and time and again, they keep on coming up with the idea that they are in contact with someone, and yes, that someone does have the characteristics of love and forgiveness and all the rest of it – now that is repeatable, and I think to myself, well, why shouldn't I trust these people that they are accurately reporting their experiences? What you look for is consensus, and when the consensus is the kind of consensus that gets distilled into the major world religions, I don't myself see why that shouldn't be accorded something of the same kind of respectability and trust as in the physical sciences.'

The obvious response here is that there is a difference to do with the potential for falsifiability. It is not at all clear what would falsify the hypothesis that prayer involves a direct experience of God.

'It is falsifiable in the individual's life,' Stannard answers. 'If I was engaged in prayer, and I became convinced that I was not in contact with anybody, if that continued, I wouldn't waste my time with it.'

But this is exactly the experience of some people, and yet it has no impact on Stannard's hypothesis, because it is trumped by his *own* personal experience, so aren't we back to unfalsifiability, I ask?

'Well,' he responds, 'there are periods when I go through a "dry patch" in terms of prayer, but one comes through it. And when you look back on those occasions, it is not always clear why you went through that dry patch. But one can only suspect that there was something wrong with one's own mindset, that one was so totally preoccupied with oneself at that time, that one loses the contact. So recognizing that there are times where my own prayer life has been flawed, that I have been putting up barriers to God, I can only presume that people who have given up on the religious life because they could not get through to God could not have been doing it properly.'

But this is precisely the difficulty. When an example is offered of the kind of thing that might falsify the claim that in prayer people are in contact with God, one finds that the claim is not falsified because it is possible to add in a caveat or rationalization – in this instance, 'well, they can't have been praying properly'. If that is always possible, then surely the hypothesis that one can enter into a direct relationship with God in prayer is not falsifiable, and therefore of a different kind to those of science?

'I think that what you have to realize,' Stannard answers, 'is that when you are talking to a religious person, they feel that they have such strong internal evidence. It's like Jung said, I don't have to believe in God, I *know* that God exists – that is how I feel. So when I come across somebody who tells me that they have tried prayer, but they have no contact, what am I supposed to say except that they must be doing something wrong?'

In *The God Experiment*, Stannard looks at a number of theological concerns and examines how science might inform how we think about them. One of these is free will, arguably a central tenet of Christian theology, because it is linked to ideas about individual responsibility, moral culpability, repentance and so on. I ask him how he reconciles his belief in free will – given that he thinks that thoughts are determined by brain events – with the apparent causal closure of the physical world, that is, the fact that physical events are wholly caused by other physical events.

'I haven't a clue,' he laughs. 'But the important point is that we have no other choice than to live our lives as though we have free will.'

But surely in theological terms more is required. One has to be committed to the idea that we actually *do* have free will, otherwise notions of guilt, repentance, sin, and so on, just dissolve. Yet they are all central to Christian theology. Wherein, for example, lies the merit of a person's repentance, if it is the inevitable product of the working out of certain physical laws?

'Well,' Stannard responds, 'that is what is so fascinating about the whole thing. One can have academic arguments like this, convince yourself that you can't possibly be free, but then what do you do – you cannot but live your life as though you do have free will.'

But surely, I press, the notion of individual responsibility requires more than the phenomenological perception of freedom, it requires that we actually *are* free. It is not fair, for example, that a person should be punished for adultery, if they were always going to be an adulterer, simply because that's how the physics worked out in their case.

'I suppose,' answers Stannard, 'that a behaviourist would say – okay, a person couldn't help but commit adultery; however, adultery is not a good thing from society's point of view, so in order to make sure that there isn't too much adultery around we will punish that person. They weren't responsible, they couldn't help it, but punishment has a desirable deterrent effect, so it is worth carrying out.'

This is a straightforward utilitarian argument, but it doesn't depend on notions of culpability, which makes it very different from any kind of Christian theological position. So the question stands, given that in scientific terms we cannot begin to explain free will, in terms of the project of *The God Experiment*, how do we get free will from the evidence?

'I just don't know,' admits Stannard, 'but I think the whole question hinges on what takes precedence, experience of life or science. I would say that the role of science is to try to explain life's experiences. One puts together an edifice of science which explains certain regularities in experience. It then seems that for some people, science, which was invented to explain experience, becomes autonomous in its own right. In the case of free will, the difficulty is that scientific conclusions seem to deny an incredibly important aspect of experience, namely, that we are free and responsible. I think it is then very doubtful to say that I am therefore wrong in taking this aspect of experience at face value. So one is placed in the situation of saying that there is something wrong with the science.'

Perhaps the least convincing section of *The God Experiment* is that which deals with the problem of evil; that is, the problem of explaining the presence of evil in a world created and sustained by a loving God. Stannard deals with this problem in a fashion fairly typical of Christian apologetics, by invoking a series of arguments, most premised on the assertion that God will create human beings with free will, which are designed to demonstrate the inevitability of evil in a world created by a *loving* God. However, to the extent that *The God Experiment* is supposed to be an evaluation of the evidence for the existence of God, wouldn't it have been more plausible, I ask him, to conclude, in line with the dictates of Ockham's razor, that the most likely explanation for the presence of evil in the world is either that there is no God or that God is not loving?

'If one was just looking at day-to-day life, and the way that people interact with each other, then I would agree with you,' he admits. 'One would come to the conclusion that if there was a deity, then at the very least it was a deity that had a shadow-side as well as a good side. But when you go beyond that – and again it's about internal experience, and also the life of Jesus – I simply can't attribute to the person I meet in my prayer life an evil side. So one is then forced into the situation of thinking, if He is not evil, what is the explanation?

'Well,' continues Stannard, 'the one characteristic that defines God, and this comes through in prayer life, is love. Now as soon as you make love the overriding principle, and not human happiness, then all sorts of tough consequences result: free will, the abuse of free will, suffering so that you have the opportunity to prove your love, all these kinds of things immediately follow.'

This is a standard response to the problem of evil. But it is easier to get a grasp on exactly what is at stake here, if one talks about specific examples. So I ask Stannard about the horrendous suffering of a child. It is interesting that in *The God Experiment*, when talking about the suffering of children, he admits that all the explanations of evil amount to nothing, if there isn't the possibility of an afterlife, which will put right the wrongs that occur during this lifetime. But in terms of weighing up the evidence for God, isn't this just the equivalent of throwing up one's hands and saying 'the arguments just don't work for children'? I put it to him that it's a cop-out.

'I can see that it would look like this to an atheist,' he concedes, 'it does seem like a cop-out. But you must think this through – would you really want an afterlife without children?'

The problem with this response is that there is a huge difference between children dying and children dying horribly.

'The afterlife absolutely has to be an integral part of any conception of a belief in a loving God,' Stannard admits. 'It does not make sense for a Christian not to believe it. It is hard to believe in the afterlife, but what is absolutely certain is that if there is not an afterlife, then the whole idea of a loving God collapses. This is something that just has to be accepted in faith, obviously we have no proof of it.'

This final answer is consistent with the others given in the interview. It is clear that, for Stannard, personal experience, and the 'knowledge' that flows from that experience, is crucial for *The God Experiment*. What this means for the scientific credibility of the experiment is a moot point. Stannard himself seems rather ambivalent about it. But perhaps that is not surprising, for arguably there is little at stake for him in the experiment, because, as he says, he doesn't have to believe in God, he *knows* that God exists.

Selected Bibliography

The God Experiment (London: Faber and Faber, 1999)

8   Science, Ethics and Society

Philosophers are often accused of squandering their talents, applying their sharp analytic skills not to the problems that most plague the world today, but to arcane puzzles largely of their own making. Those who make such accusations would readily admit that there are a few philosophers for whom even such a *prima facie* case against them fails. These are the moral philosophers who have served on various commissions and committees, advising governments and professional organizations on matters of great ethical concern.

Mary Warnock, who chaired the commission on human fertilization and embryology in the early 1980s, is the most well-known of these philosophers in Britain. Today, one of the most prominent philosophers in this sphere is Professor John Harris of Manchester University. Throughout his career he has been active in the field of bioethics, perhaps the most practically important branch of philosophy today. He was one of the founder directors of the International Association of Bioethics and a founder member of the board of the Journal *Bioethics*. He has acted as an ethical consultant to bodies such as the European Parliament, the World Health Organisation, the European Commission, the Joint United Nations Programme on HIV/AIDS (UNAIDS), the United Kingdom Department of Health, the Health Council of the Netherlands, the Research Council of Norway, and Granada Television.

He has sat on the ethics committee of the British Medical Association, on and off, for around ten years, helping to advise the profession and set its policy. He also served on the governmental advisory committee on genetic testing, which at the end of 1999, with Harris still serving, evolved into the Human Genetics Commission (HGC). In 2001 he became the first philosopher to be elected a fellow of the Academy of Medical Sciences, by way of recognition of this broad range of contributions to the field.

In much of his work, especially on committees, Harris is working alongside scientists, clinicians, people from industry and consumer groups, and people with personal knowledge of genetic illness and disability. So what happens when an academic philosopher enters the fray of real-life ethical decision-making? If we were to take the allegory of Plato's cave seriously, we might expect it to be like a descent into intellectual darkness, away from the clear light of philosophical meditation. If, on the other hand, we were to take philosophy's critics seriously, we might expect it to be like asking a theoretical physicist to mend your fuse box.

Reality, fortunately, does not conform to either stereotype. The picture Harris paints is of a collaborative exercise, where the philosopher fulfils one role among many, neither first among equals nor too far removed from the job at hand.

'I think it's important to have philosophical representation on such committees because philosophers do have some skills which, while others may have them, you can be sure philosophers do,' he explained. 'Those skills are in terms of both the analysis of argument, and its articulation and presentation. I think that it's very important to bear in mind that philosophers aren't good just at articulating and presenting their own arguments, but also at actually formulating arguments for others, even if they don't necessarily agree with them. So one of the roles of philosophers on such committees is to help the committee and individual members of it to say what they want to say with clarity and precision. Of course, philosophers aren't unique in being able to do that, but they are, as it were, professionally qualified to do it.'

One advantage Harris would seem to have is that he is able to draw on a large resource of knowledge about ethics and moral philosophy which a lot of his fellow committee members do not have. Isn't that an impairment to their ability to do a good job?

'I don't think it is,' he firmly replies, 'because we're all contributing different things, and as long as there is somebody there who can, for example, articulate clearly issues of autonomy, or whatever, I don't think others need to do that. They can provide what I lack, which is detailed scientific knowledge; or in some cases detailed knowledge of social science research, of how to consult the public without prejudging the issues; or about how the operation of something like our own system, the National Health Service, is going to effect the delivery of therapies and preventive strategies. It's no good us recommending something if there's no chance, given the way the health care system is structured, of getting where it is we want to go.'

Their deliberations are, Harris is pleased to say, 'not at all like academic seminars, not simply because philosophy seminars are designed either to help educate students or to get at the philosophically right or best answer to a particular problem. These committees are rightly not trying to do either of those things. Our ultimate responsibility is to advise government. But we advise government on a range of things, perhaps least of all on what they ought to do, since that is not our business. We advise government on the issues, the possible dangers and on possible solutions to problems. We also have to understand what the public's concerns, fears and views are, and sometimes to take cognizance of those in our deliberations. So it's very unlike a philosophy seminar or meeting.'

Would he say that the purposes of moral philosophy are different from the purposes of an ethics committee?

'I'm not sure what the purposes of moral philosophy are, to be honest,' he replies. 'A shameful thing for a moral philosopher to admit, but I'm not sure that it has purposes. There is a whole range of things which broadly come under the umbrella of ethics, only some of which are moral philosophy, and only some of the moral philosophy ones are relevant to committees like this.'

One difference between his committee work and moral philosophy is that what is up for grabs at the committees is more limited than it is in philosophy. 'Take two issues,' Harris explains, 'neither of which is being considered by any of the committees I'm on at the moment: xenografting – animal tissue into humans – and human reproductive cloning. Both of those are important public issues and at the moment one fact about both of them means that they're not on the agenda, and that is that neither of those processes is considered safe. Once you know that, in a way, there's nothing further to discuss ethically. It resolves all the other issues, because no one is gong to recommend something which isn't safe.'

'We also need to be cognizant of the fact that we're not starting with a clean sheet,' he adds later, when we move on to discuss ethical issues concerning embryos. 'We're starting in a society which has already decided certain things about the embryo. For example, we're operating in a society which permits abortion, under various acts of parliament. So we're operating in a context where that particular question is already determined and we're not able to readdress that. Even though one member of the commission may be broadly in favour of abortion and another broadly against it, that issue doesn't arise, because we have to operate in a society where that question has already been answered. That very often is the line taken. One of the things that constrains what we might do is what, if you like, the people, through parliament, have already decided.

'A very good example of that is something not addressed by our commission, but which was addressed very recently by another committee the government set up. The Chief Medical Officer's expert group on stem cell research recommended approval of extending permission to experiment on early embryos in order to obtain embryonic stem cells. It did that largely on the grounds of consistency, namely that, after the Warnock committee, the Human Fertilisation and Embryology Act (1990) already permitted experimentation on human embryos up to fourteen days for fertility purposes. They said that is a fact that we can't revisit. The question people anyway. You have to address issues that people can relate to without a lot of background.'

Sitting on an ethics committee opens one up to the accusation of being part of a selected elite who are there to act as our moral guardians. There's an unwelcome paternalistic air around them. Is that something which Harris is concerned about?

'I think it's a misunderstanding of our role,' he replies. 'If I thought we were an elite group of guardians of public morality I wouldn't join the committee, or I certainly wouldn't stay on it once I'd found that out. Our job is a complicated one, but it's essentially to analyse a whole range of evidence and argument and advise the government accordingly. The government is under no obligation to take our advice, even if and when we're in a position to clearly offer any. We're not a regulatory body.'

The involvement of people like Harris in ethics committees is heartening, not only because it points up a way in which philosophers can contribute directly to society, but also because it shows that moral philosophy can be of use even though moral philosophers are far from agreeing about the nature, purpose and fundamentals of ethics. While work in that area carries on in the academy, there is still plenty that can be said in the live ethical debates that so concern us all.

Selected Bibliography

Violence and Responsibility (London: Routledge, 1980)

The Value of Life (London: Routledge, 1985)

Wonderwoman and Superman: Ethics and Human Biotechnology (Oxford: Oxford University Press, 1992)

Biomedical Ethics: Oxford Readings in Philosophy Series, ed. (Oxford: Oxford University Press, 2001)

A Companion to Genetics: Philosophy and the Genetic Revolution, ed. with Justine C. Burley (Oxford: Blackwell, 2000)

III   Religion

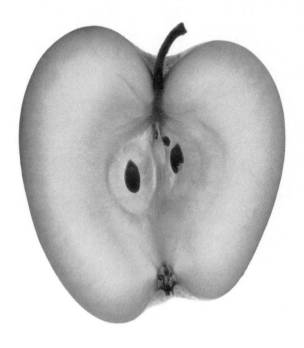

9   The Non-realist God

Don Cupitt

There is a Cambridge don who believes that 'it's obvious that gods embody cultural values and ideals' and that 'belief in a superior, invisible order of reality' doesn't make sense. He doesn't 'think any religious beliefs are literally true' and is 'inclined to think now that we've probably got to drop the word [god]'. To round things off, he also does not believe religion is necessary.

You might be forgiven for thinking this man is anti-religious, an atheist for sure. And indeed, many orthodox believers claim that he is both these things. But the person in question denies the accusations. Don Cupitt, the non-realist theologian, is not just religious, he's an ordained Anglican minister.

When Cupitt entered the ministry in Manchester in 1959 he was an orthodox theist, committed to a belief in the independent existence of a loving, personal God. Over the years, however, Cupitt became increasingly unable to reconcile traditional theism with what we know about ourselves and the world today. Cupitt's God remained real, but a human creation, not a transcendent reality.

Cupitt has been promoting his non-realist interpretation of religion for nearly thirty years now. In the 1980s, his BBC television series and book, *The Sea of Faith*, brought his sophisticated, intellectual reading of religion to a wide, and widely uncomprehending, audience. Cupitt thought he and people like him could change the Church, bring belief up to date and make it fit to inhabit the modern world. The Sea of Faith network was born with high hopes of turning the ebbing tide of religious belief by making faith commensurable with a modern world-view. Its short mission statement encapsulates Cupitt's own core beliefs: 'The Network explores the implications of accepting religion as a human creation; promotes this view of religion, and affirms the continuing validity of religious thought and practice as celebrations of spiritual and social values.'

Twenty years and dozens of books on, little has changed and Cupitt has begun to despair of the Church, which has in no uncertain terms told Cupitt and his ilk that it didn't need his kind of modernization. In ecclesiastical eyes, what Cupitt calls religion is atheism by any other name. The iconoclastic fellow of Emmanuel College continues to write and think, but he is as marginal to mainstream religion as ever.

Cupitt is a doubly puzzling figure. First, his non-realist conception of God is difficult to comprehend. But then, once one has got some grasp of what his view is, there is the puzzle of why it should be called religion at all.

To understand Cupitt's positive thesis, it's important to see the negative one. Just what is Cupitt against?

'I was initially prompted by reaction against the views of Richard Swinburne,' explains Cupitt, 'who seems to treat God as an empirical hypothesis to account for various features of the world. I don't think the hypothesis can be made clear enough. I don't think the mechanism by which God works can be spelt out with a scientific kind of precision.'

What Cupitt finds incomprehensible is the idea that God is some kind of really existent entity. For him, that idea only makes sense if one is trapped in an out-moded, Platonic form of thinking. 'I think Platonism – belief in a second, invisible world or order of being alongside the world of experience – has affected people very deeply,' he explains, 'and it helps them go on believing in things like life after death or a metaphysical God, or even in objective moral values. But none of those beliefs, to my mind, makes any sense at all once we before us is whether there is any reason not to extend the principles enshrined there beyond fertility research into stem cell research.'

Despite these important differences in how the various bioethical bodies and moral philosophy work, what the committees do is not so different from what Harris does in applied philosophy, particularly bioethics or medical ethics. 'I find a lot of what I do as a bioethicist, as a particular sort of hybrid philosopher, is rather like what we do in these committees, in the sense that a lot of what I do as a bioethicist is gathering information: scientific information, information about what technologies do and what biological processes do, what drugs do, and actually thinking about the ethics of all of that. That is, in a way, what our committee does. It considers a vast range of information about what's going on in science and medicine and technology, and then it tries to analyse all of that in terms of what benefits and burdens that might represent for the community.'

The interface between academic moral philosophy and the work of the committees is a complex and interesting one. In one sense, the work involves you in 'constantly re-inventing the wheel, because most of the issues go back to some very basic stuff in philosophy, in reconciling the entitlements and rights of individuals against the needs of the community, something very basic like that, or in actually analysing autonomy to show that autonomy doesn't just mean doing what you want. It means doing what you want with limitations about the health and safety and autonomy of others and so on. So very often the philosophical part of what one is doing is actually fairly basic but still very necessary.'

However, in some cases the philosophy is simply irrelevant. 'Cloning, arising from the birth of Dolly, was a classic example, because people had not thought that would be possible for scientific reasons, and suddenly it happened. There was huge misunderstanding of the science involved and what cloning meant. People had this idea you'd have Xerox copies of existing people churned out. But they also lacked a perspective from which to think about the ethics of it. They knew it was disquieting and a lot of people didn't like the idea of it.

But in trying to articulate their fears and disquiet, a whole range of classic philosophical objections came up, which were interesting because in a way they were beside the point, because the objections didn't sensibly apply to the case that people thought they did.

'To take one example: a lot of the reaction to cloning centred on the undesirability of there existing two copies of the same genome, without remembering that identical twins are just that. So a lot of people said that people's individuality would be undermined, or their dignity would be threatened, or they would be conditioned by the life of this other person. In the whole of human history we have a wonderful example of how to deal with this and all of that was somehow forgotten.'

This aspect is important, since in the popular press and television news, much of the time when these bioethical stories break, there does seem to be a lot of ignorance about what is actually going on. To what extent is it the case that once people become properly informed, it's much easier to articulate a coherent moral position on a given issue?

'I think public information is hugely important,' says Harris, 'and one of the roles of the committees is public information. That's a very difficult role to discharge, because to embark on a programme of public education is very expensive. But it's certainly part of our remit to provide information. That is hugely important. I think there are two public information issues. One is the huge misunderstandings the public have concerning genetics. If you take the genetically modified organisms issue, there is a wide feeling that naturally farmed products don't have genes in them, that genes only come in when there's something bad coming in. The other education or information issue is that a lot of scientists are very ignorant about ethical issues. So there are two issues: educating the public about science and educating the scientists in particular about ethics and to a certain extent about law.'

There is also, presumably, a need to educate the moral philosophers who take part in these debates about the science too.

'Certainly. I'm somebody who has a classic humanities background. I actually read philosophy and English literature at university to start with, so I have no scientific background at all. I had to acquire a very incomplete scientific education in a very informal way, mostly by having worked a lot of my life in a very large university with a lot of good scientists. I've been able to talk to scientists at the cutting edge and learn from them, which has been a major advantage.'

One thing that becomes clear talking to Harris is that applied philosophy is a much more complex matter than simply applying philosophical theories of ethics to real-world problems.

'When I produce arguments in the committee I'm not saying to myself, "Is this consistent with the particular version of consequentialism which I think is the best available moral theory?" I'm using the fact that I have worked out the particular conception of consequentialism over the years which I think gives the best approach. But I'm not saying this is right because a particular brand of preference utilitarianism I favour requires it. I'm saying these are the reasons that seem to sustain this conclusion, and then others will produce other considerations. In many ways consequentialism is a quite useful approach, since it doesn't carry a huge amount of baggage that needs to be explained. It appeals to things that people by and large intuitively accept, like the importance of avoiding pain and getting better outcomes. You don't have to articulate a very complicated metaphysical system in order to get going.'

However, members of the committee do not need to share a particular moral outlook in order to make progress, make decisions and in many cases reach consensus. How is that possible?

'I think it's possible to appeal broadly to rational principles in committees like this. You often don't have to articulate the underpinnings of those rational principles since they are widely accepted, even though people might have different bases for them. Take a completely uncontentious issue, such as that killing the innocent is wrong. I don't know of a moral theory that has a divergent view on that. So if you were a Kantian, a consequentialist or an Aristotelian you would have that belief. You would articulate its defence in different ways. Very often, the sorts of issues which one is dealing with are things by and large where decent people broadly agree.

'I'm actually encouraged by the fact that we have a number of different religions and certainly a wide variety of different moral viewpoints on the committee, that on the whole, although we disagree on details, we achieve a remarkable consensus on broad approaches, and also, I must say, a remarkable amount of respect for one another. Although there are hugely divergent views on the committee, there is a vast amount of mutual respect and you never get into the kind of sarcastic put downs that characterize philosophy seminars. People have huge respect for one another's views and even if they can see flaws with them, are very patient about how they point out those flaws and how they try to build on the elements of agreement that exist.'

'Let me give you an example. Take the conjoined twins case. I've appeared on a number of television and radio programmes on this and I find myself in total agreement on the practical outcome with people that I would normally disagree with very fundamentally, namely representatives of life lobbies, because, although our fundamental principles are totally different and on many things we would be absolutely divergent, we came to the same view for quite different reasons. In a way, the reasons were only articulated in broad terms, but the way they got articulated sounded very similar, namely that we felt a lot of respect was due to the beliefs of the parents and for very different reasons, we felt that although there were arguments in favour of separating the twins, they weren't conclusive arguments.

'If I'm talking about the conjoined twins, I don't start by saying you've got to decide the moral status of infants and address the question of whether they are persons or not, or whether they're self-conscious. If you go into that you're going to lose ninety per cent of

motivating side of oneself. A personal God is the same sort of object as a person's ideal, dream or ambition. That is to say, gods always belong to people – there are no free-floating gods.'

One difficulty with this view is that to say all knowledge is a human construct is ambiguous, the meaning of which can range from the uncontroversial to the preposterous. Relatively uncontroversially, Cupitt maintains, 'we're always inside our own point of view, our own culture, our own language, our own interests'. Yet he also says, more problematically, that 'scientific theories are not discoveries but inventions'. Cupitt is quite insistent on this point.

'We made all the theories. Physics didn't fall out of the sky, Darwin didn't discover the theory of evolution, he invented it and it works. That is to say, we have produced among ourselves, through our conversation, all the general categories and theories in terms of which we organize and interpret our experience. If we were deprived of all these habits of interpretation we would be in the position of new-born babies for whom there's nothing but a confusing bombardment of stimuli. All meaning is produced by us, all truth is produced by us. From that point of view I agree with the thorough-going post-modernists – we make it all. The world is a huge collection of communally evolved customs of interpretation.'

However, Cupitt is aware that adhering to such a post-modernist viewpoint does not entail an 'anything goes' attitude. He accepts that tarot is not equivalent to quantum physics, or astrology equivalent to astronomy. 'There is still a difference between consistency and inconsistency, and between what works and what doesn't work.'

This difference does mean that certain types of knowledge, such as scientific knowledge, fall into a different category to imaginative, creative work. There has to be a correspondence between the theory and our experience – all within the realm of the human – for a scientific theory to stand up. So we can say the theory of evolution is invented, but the reason why it survives is because it matches experience, experience confirms it time and again. At this point Cupitt insists that he is not going back to empiricism and the correspondence theory of truth. As he sees it, our experience is always formed by our theories and therefore seems to confirm them. This is significant, because when Cupitt says all knowledge is humanly created, the suggestion is that one needn't be worried or surprised that so too is religion. But there is nonetheless an important difference between scientific knowledge and artistic creation, so once we realize that religion is really on the side of the artist and not on the side of the scientist, doesn't that threaten the seriousness of religion?

'Let me point out there a difference between science and art,' explains Cupitt. 'In science it's a good thing to have an academy to maintain professional discipline, so that everybody uses a standard vocabulary and standard mathematical procedures, and constructs their world in the same sort of way. But in art it's much more important to find your own voice, so vocabularies, ways of world-building, differ. The artist puts more emphasis on emotional expression, building a world that gives a feel that you can respond to emotionally. The scientist puts more emphasis on mathematical organization, making experience routinized and therefore intelligible, putting patterns into experience. So the scientist builds a rule-governed world, the artist builds a world which we respond to, a world our hearts can go out to.

'I would say that the human being's need for routine and a knowable world is one thing, but an equally great need is the need to express ourselves symbolically. Art, theatre, music and all those things are about our need to go out into expression, in order to become ourselves. We are not ready-made selves, we become selves by expressing ourselves in our lives. So whereas science tends to play down subjectivity, religion and art strongly emphasize it. In religion and art we want to come out, strut our stuff and do our thing and become ourselves. In science we want to see the world as intelligible and rule-governed. It's a different ambition.'

This viewpoint provides an intellectually coherent justification for a 'pick and mix' approach to religion. 'In my view,' explains Cupitt, 'religion is more like art than science, so it's quite all right to admire and learn from more than one religion just as it's perfectly okay to admire and learn from more than one different style of painting. We live in an age of extreme pluralism in art styles, and we're quite used to that. Why shouldn't we similarly admire both Buddhism and Christianity, as I do? The idea that a religion is a kind of nationalism and that it has to be exclusive and if you belong to one you must regard all the others as potential enemies is out of date.'

Yet the nagging doubt remains: if this is all religion is, why call it religion at all? Cupitt seems quite happy to drop a lot of religious vocabulary. Of the word 'God', he says 'I'm inclined to think now that we've probably got to drop the word because it's got so many misleading associations. It's used to justify so much cruelty, ignorance and fanaticism that I often feel reluctant to use it.'

I put it to him that, given that religious language carries with it a lot of historical baggage, there's a risk of bad faith in persisting with the old religious vocabulary. Wouldn't it be more honest, and, in terms of changing society, more constructive, to just dispense with all talk of God and prayer, given all the associations that go with them?

'In the last few years I've been inclined to say that,' he agreed, 'because I've had no success at all in persuading the Church that my account of God is worth taking seriously. It's about the same as Kant's, by the way. The view of God that I put forward in 1980, in *Taking Leave of God*, is about the same as Kant's. Kant kept God as an ideal about which we could speak in symbolic terms. But people won't accept that. They say "Cupitt's an atheist" and dismiss my ideas. So I'd be inclined now to go independent of the Church and try to engage in a kind of experimental, creative religious writing that I hope will be useful in the future. For me there is no compulsory religious vocabulary.'

Cupitt seems to be, above all, a man who wants to dispense with all of religion's claims to truth, yet who sees something in religion that is worth preserving. He articulated some of this feeling when he contrasted his religiosity with the atheism of Sartre.

'I sometimes quote there the contrast between Sartre's atheism and the religious attitude of a British philosopher like Ernest Gellner, who was certainly no theist and no religious believer. But he did tell me, "I have a religious attitude to life." He wondered at life, he felt there was something there that deserved our respect and acknowledgement, just in the flow of life itself. He didn't like either the Marxist or the atheist existentialist view of the individual human being as a purely sovereign positer of values and organizer of the world. One needs to have a sort of to-and-fro, a dialectic between the self and life. I have suggested that in today's thinking the word "life" has taken on much of the religious significance that the word God used to have.'

When you strip away from religion all the excess baggage that Cupitt believes needs removing, this seems to be at the core of what remains. Cupitt describes this attitude as 'love of life, a kind of moral responsiveness to existence, no more than that, trying to get away from a rather aggressively masculine, Sartrean imperialism of the will. To my mind that runs too close to fascism and the aggressive humanism of the 1930s. I'm not happy with that morally. I prefer English religious humanism, which is linked with the weakness of Christ, with the poor and with human suffering rather than with power.'

It is for this reason that he says 'religious virtues and values continue to be interesting and important'. Commenting on some remarks by Prime Minister Tony Blair on the importance of religious values, he observed Blair 'did not say that religious doctrinal beliefs should play a part in our lives, nor would any serious politician say that'. Religious values without religious doctrine – that is what Cupitt wants for the twenty-first century.

I wondered in what sense religion could still be a source of values if we accept that all values are human-made. 'Žižeck makes the point here by arguing that, contrary to the rationalist tradition, human thinking is very often heterological rather than purely autonomous,' Cupitt explains. 'We don't just think up our values and impose them on experience. Rather our thinking is always prompted by things out there, and persons who think for us. It's no accident that celebrity endorsement and celebrity opinion is nowadays needed for English people to take any idea at all seriously. We think through various kinds of proxies, symbols and ideas. Very few people are purely sovereign and autonomous creative thinkers in a post-Cartesian individualist way. Most of us work through myths, through other people, through values derived from religion.

'Let me take humanitarianism as an example. Christianity is a religion which, with Judaism, parented our modern humanitarian ethics and it did historically need people slowly to get the idea of compassion for the suffering of Christ, and then to start caring about their fellow human beings. Humanitarianism has been a very latent, slow and laborious development. It still hasn't fully arrived. It's an ethic which needs a symbol of human suffering and weakness as being itself religiously significant to start it off.

'So I want to say,' he continues, 'religion supplies us with poetry and myths to live by, and human beings need stories to live by. Because our existence is temporal we've always got to construct some kind of story of our lives, and that story, to my mind, needs to have a religious quality. So I don't think any religious beliefs are literally true, but I think they're all existentially or morally useful, or a great many of them are.'

However, once again, Cupitt is prepared to allow that a religious viewpoint is not strictly necessary. 'In my religious universe there's no authoritative system of dogma, so I'm quite happy that non-religious people, if they can make their point of view make sense, should have their say. I don't believe in any orthodoxy any more.'

Religion without doctrine, religion without creed, religion without belief in another, spiritual world, distinct from the world we live in – that is what Cupitt is striving for. Is religion without all these things still religion? It's a question a serious engagement with Cupitt's thought forces you to consider. Whether you call it religion or not, Cupitt is trying to show us the precious baby sitting in the now rather dirty bathwater of traditional religion. What we call it is neither here nor there; what matters is whether or not we should be saving it.

Selected Bibliography

The Sea of Faith, 2nd edn (London: SCM Press, 1994)
After God: The Future of Religion (New York: Basic Books, 1997)
Philosophy's Own Religion (London: SCM Press, 2000)
Taking Leave of God, 2nd edn (London: SCM Press, 2001)
Emptiness and Brightness (Santa Rosa: Polebridge Press, 2002)

10 Freedom and Evil

Richard Swinburne

Prisoners of war are usually commanded to give their captors no more than their name, rank and serial number. Reticent academics similarly make few details of their non-professional lives public, and offer only name, position and bibliography.

In the case of Richard Swinburne, these details perhaps tell us all we need to know. He is the Nolloth Professor of the Philosophy of the Christian Religion at the University of Oxford and has published many books, such as *The Existence of God*, *Is There a God?*, *Revelation*, *Miracles*, *The Coherence of Theism*, *The Christian God*, *Providence and the Problem of Evil*, *Faith and Reason*, *The Resurrection of God Incarnate* and *The Evolution of the Soul*. In other words, Richard Swinburne's life has been dedicated to showing that Christian religious belief is philosophically respectable and that arguments from the existence of the universe, its orderliness, the existence of human beings and suchlike make it probable that there is a God.

This is no easy task, since in contemporary academic philosophy traditional theists are in a minority. In this hostile environment, most theistic philosophers have to spend a long time doing apologetics – making a defensive case for the compatibility of religious belief with the wider findings of reason and experience.

This requires some dirty work on the part of the pious philosopher and perhaps the dirtiest of all is justifying why it is that, although we live in a universe created and governed by an all-good, all-powerful God, nasty things happen. While the good shepherd rules over us, people are subject to torture, slow-death and misery by their fellow men, while disease, floods and hurricanes can leave whole nations on their knees, a seething mass of misery and pain.

This apparent contradiction between the benevolence of God and the cruelty of the world is usually referred to as the problem of evil. Swinburne has examined the problem more thoroughly than perhaps anyone else working on the problem today. His attempt to construct a theodicy – a way of reconciling the co-existence of a good God and evil – puts sharply into relief just how hard the task of the apologist is. Not that Swinburne is entirely happy with the word 'evil'.

'I don't think it's a very happy word to use, because in ordinary English, evil isn't just a bad state of affairs, it's a wicked act somebody does, and hence we have the moral principle that you shouldn't do evil so that good may occur. That's the natural, ordinary language use of evil. But I don't wish to pin myself to that by using the word "evil". I simply mean by evil an intrinsically bad state of affairs, such as suffering.'

Swinburne spoke to me on the occasion of his talk on God and evil given at the twentieth World Congress of Philosophy. His paper set out four requirements that, if met, reconcile the existence of God and the existence of evil, and if not, leave the two in contradiction. As evil – understood as bad states of affairs – exists as surely as day and night, this would amount to a rejection of the existence of God.

These conditions are that only by allowing evil can good be achieved; that God does everything else he can to bring about that good; that the person allowing the evil, in this case God, has the right to allow the evil; and that the outcome has to be sufficiently good.

Swinburne sees the first condition as necessary, 'because evil is evil. That is to say pain and suffering are the sorts of things that good people do not allow to happen, or if they can easily prevent it, do not allow to happen unless there's some reason why they should allow it to happen; in other words, that some good is served by it. God is above all the creator of the universe who not merely allows evil to happen, but provides an environment in which either he brings it about or allows somebody else to bring it about, and unless there's a good purpose for which he allows this to happen, it seems our understanding of "good" is such that he would be less than good if he allowed us to suffer agony and there wasn't any point in it.'

The problem with this is that some argue that the allowing of evil to bring about some other good undermines the goodness in itself. There are some goods which it seems aren't worth attaining if it requires there to be an evil to bring them about.

'Your point is, is the good worth the pain?' replies Swinburne. 'Well, that depends on what the good is; my other conditions have to be satisfied. I gave two or three examples in the paper of how certain good states couldn't be attained without a necessary evil, and since it is God that we're talking about, the good has to be a logical good – God being omnipotent can do anything logically possible. He can produce any good without producing evil unless it's logically necessary that the evil should occur in order that the good should occur. I gave two or three examples of where that is the case.

'For example, it's a good thing that humans should have free will, not just free will to choose between alternative television channels, but free will to choose significantly between good and bad – good and evil in the terms of the paper. But they can't have that unless there is the actual possibility of them bringing about evil. The possibility of evil occurring unprevented is the necessary condition for them having a free choice between good and evil.'

This is a version of the so-called free-will defence for the existence of evil. One major objection to it is that the way God created the universe does place some restrictions on our freedom because of the way we are. We are not free to fly, for example. Could not God have arranged the world such that, though we had the possibility to choose between good and evil, there was nonetheless something about the world that prevented us from doing some of the really awful terrible things that happen in the world?

'Yes, he could,' allows Swinburne, 'and here one must distinguish different degrees of freedom he could give us. First of all, as I say, he could just give us freedom to choose between goods, but that wouldn't be a particularly valuable freedom. A more significant freedom is the freedom to choose between good and bad. Now what if the only sorts of bad he would allow us to do were extremely limited? For instance, he could allow us to cause mild pain to other people, but not seriously to wreck their future. He would be like the over-protective parent who is not really going to give their child freedom, only a nominal freedom which only makes a tiny difference, but this isn't really handing over any significant control. There is a pay-off here – if God is to give us significant control then there has to be the possibility of really significant bad.'

The importance of free will also comes out in the second condition. God has to give us the maximum opportunity to achieve the good which his permitting of evil allows. To do this, he must make us free.

'Suppose that he allows us to suffer pain in order that we may have the opportunity to deal with it freely in a courageous way or not to deal with it freely in a courageous way. If we are to deal with our pain in a courageous way or not deal with it in a courageous way, clearly we've got to have the pain. Although that would justify the pain, suppose God doesn't do everything else to promote the good, because he doesn't actually give us free will. In that case, there wouldn't be any point to the pain, unless he gave us the free will as well in order that we may choose how to deal with it. That's the point of that clause.'

So far, Swinburne's argument hinges on the necessity of allowing free choice and hence the possibility of people causing real harm. But what about the misery which is not caused by free choice, such as disease and flooding, so-called 'natural evil'? How is that justified?

'I think there are different kinds of natural evil and I would give different theodicies for each,' replies Swinburne, selecting one example from the many found in his work. 'Human suffering as the result of disease – very frequent, not the result of free choice, or at any rate not the result of free choice unless there are bad angels at work causing it. That is possible, but it's not something I would wish to promote very strongly. That sort of suffering is necessary because it gives the sufferer the opportunity to either be sorry for himself or to deal with it courageously. If he didn't suffer he wouldn't have the opportunity to deal with his suffering in either a courageous way or in a self-pitying way. It also gives other people – friends, spouse, children and so on – the opportunity to be sympathetic, to try and help him, for showing sympathy, feeling sympathy and doing something about it or not to bother. That is to say, this is the grit that makes possible the pearl of different kinds of reaction. If the world were without any natural evil and suffering we wouldn't have the opportunity, or nearly as much opportunity, to show courage, patience and sympathy. Of course I'm not suggesting that God ought to multiply suffering *ad infinitum* in order to give us endless opportunity, but I do think the world would be a poorer place if we didn't have some opportunity to show ourselves at our best in this kind of way.'

But does God have the right to allow the evil, as the third condition requires? Swinburne claims he does, and offers an illustration of why. 'There may be some street kid who is a nuisance. I may reason that if I beat the child, the child will reform and not be a nuisance any more. On the other hand, it's not my child and I don't have the right to go about beating children just because I think it will do them good. That is to say, one can't justify allowing evil to occur or imposing it simply in terms of it having good consequences. One has got to have the right to cause this to somebody, and that's very important. The question inevitably arises as to why God has this right.

'God does have this right because you have to be in a kind of parental situation with regard to somebody else if you are to cause suffering or allow them to suffer. The reason for that is that you are overall their benefactor. You've given them life, nourishment, education and so on and therefore you have the right to demand certain things in return. Certain things which the creator demands in return may require some suffering. As long as that's in a good cause, that's fine enough. [One] can send a child to a neighbourhood school even though the child isn't going to be very happy there for the sake of cementing relations in the community. So of course a parent does have the right to demand something in return from the child if necessary by way of suffering because of the great good one confers on the child.'

I suggest to Swinburne that someone just doesn't have the right to inflict or allow suffering on a person merely because they have given them in the past and will continue to give them in the future certain goods, even if the harm is for the person's own benefit. To give someone some goods does not in any way give you an authority over that person.

'In the case of an adult,' replies Swinburne, 'if we give them something and they don't accept it then there is no relationship established. But if they do accept it then I think they commit themselves to a certain minor obligation to doing you a favour in return if you ask it. I understand that you might dispute this, so look at it bringing in this extra crucial factor: God has to make the universe without consulting us about what sort of universe we would like to be in because we're not there to be consulted.' Swinburne compares this to examples in medical ethics.

'The times doctors have to take decisions about the well-being of patients who are in no condition to take those decisions themselves, they say, "what should I do that is in the best interests of the patient?" That's not the only consideration. They may say, "I have obligations to other patients as well. So it would be wrong of me as a doctor to do everything for the one patient at the expense of any other of the patients, and I must take that into account."

'So, analogously, God the father, creating the universe, considers what is for the good of each of us, but bearing in mind that he can only provide some goods for each of us if he doesn't provide total goods for others of us. But he's got on balance to provide goods for each of us and that indeed is the system. That is to say there are limits to what God can demand from us by way of suffering. The package of life he gives us as a whole must be good.

'That is where the central point of my paper comes in, that it is a good for an individual to be of use for others, and that's not just a good for others, it is a good for *me* if I am of use for others. Of course, ideally, I choose to be a good to others, but not only if I choose to be a good *for* others. If in some sense I have to be a use to others, so long as I'm not rebelling against it, if voluntarily by my actions I am a good for others, that's a benefit for me and it's also a benefit for me if my life is used to the benefit of others. I brought out several examples of that, of which, of course, the most striking would be the person who dies for his country in a just war, leading it is hoped to ultimate victory. But even if he's a conscript, every society except our own recognizes that that wasn't merely a good for other people, it was a good for him that his life was of tremendous use to everybody else.'

The obvious rejoinder to this is that so much suffering seems to be not just useless for the sufferer, but useless to anyone else, or at the very least not valuable enough to even begin to justify it. As an example, I gave those who died in the battle of the Somme, a mass slaughter of conscripts which served no strategic benefit.

'Well, that particular soldier's life is also of use, but not in the way I have just described. That is to say, taking this example, someone sent him there, some general high up has taken a decision about this matter. The war hasn't just happened, it's been the result of all sorts of decisions and all sorts of acts of negligence by politicians on both sides, all sorts of lack of preaching a gospel of love by churches on both sides – innumerable people, through negligence, through stirring up hatred, through not bothering, have contributed to war.

'It's a great good for them that they are allowed to make big differences to things, and they can only make big differences to things if there are going to be possible victims. That is to say, it's only because some people will suffer if they make the wrong decision that the possibility of big wrong decisions is open to them. And so the soldier on the Somme, his life is of use because by its availability he makes the possibility of big decisions open to many, many other people.' And remember that, according to Swinburne, it's 'not just a good for others, it is a good for me if I am of use for others'.

Hearing all this, some have responded not by questioning the logic of the defence, but with a moral repugnance about what it all entails. If this is a God who really believes that it is good for people to suffer terribly for other people, and that it is also good for them, then that God is not worthy of our worship. Swinburne thinks the distaste can be eased by a sense of perspective.

'One of the very important things you're doing with a theodicy is taking into account other aspects of the Christian package, or the package of any other religion. One very obvious and important thing is that life only lasts seventy or eighty years on earth, but for most religions, including the Christian one, that is as a small drop in eternity and what we are doing in this world is making choices which affect the sort of person we are to be and therefore the sort of life we are capable of enjoying in the next world, whether we're in the right relation to God or not. God is interested not merely in us living a comfortable life in this world, which is of course in itself a good thing, but on a bigger scale God is interested in us being heroes and making heroic total commitments in difficult circumstances. If we do, we form a character which makes us the kind of people who will be capable of enjoying the beatific vision of heaven.'

Swinburne makes very clear what reconciling God and evil requires. Two things in particular it requires is that God has the right to inflict that suffering and that it is justifiable to allow something very terrible indeed for a greater good. I put it to Swinburne that many will find this hard to swallow.

'If somebody thinks that the only good things in the world are kicks of pleasure and the only bad things are stabs of pain, this isn't going to have any immediate effect. But I like to think that most people aren't in that situation and that they do see some other somewhat more complicated things as rather good and somewhat more complicated things as rather bad. The examples that I started with in this conversation and in my book are non-theological examples, cases where we admit that parents have certain rights over children, states have certain rights over their citizens, that it's a good for me if I am of benefit for others. I say to people, well let's take this a bit seriously. If you do take it seriously, perhaps there's rather more to be said for these moral views than we thought to start with, and I hope to be persuasive, but it does involve producing many, many examples.'

Swinburne had already said that his argument wouldn't immediately convince the committed atheist and wouldn't make much difference to the committed believer. Reconciling God and evil is of most value to the undecided or unsure. The question we are left with is whether the very precise reconciliation Swinburne describes will have the effect of clearing the way for belief in God or making the very idea of God a more chilling one.

Selected Bibliography

The Coherence of Theism (Oxford: Clarendon Press, 1977)
The Existence of God (Oxford: Oxford University Press, 1991)
Is There a God? (Oxford: Oxford University Press, 1996)
Providence and the Problem of Evil (Oxford: Oxford University Press, 1998)
The Resurrection of God Incarnate (Oxford: Oxford University Press, 2003)

11 Philosophy of Religion

Peter Vardy

Not many philosophers have on their CVs fellowships of the Institute of Chartered Accountants and the Institute of Marketing and directorships or chairs of companies listed on the London Stock Exchange. Peter Vardy does, but once you've met him, the incongruity soon fades.

Peter Vardy is quite simply a whirlwind. Having greeted me at his college, he sets off to make us coffee, leaving me puffing in his wake. Pirouetting around the kitchen, I am given the most genuinely instant coffee I have ever had. Trying not to spill anything, we hurl ourselves into the common room for our chat.

Vardy chats as he moves – quickly, nimbly and with boundless energy. All of a sudden, you begin to wonder why his *Puzzle* series of books on philosophy, aimed at a wide readership, only numbers five. Surely this man could knock one off in a weekend.

This boundless energy is reflected in his entrepreneurship and makes sense of his business past. Vardy is not just interested in ideas, he's interested in doing things and communicating. His use of Power Point presentations in lectures – a staple in the business world but still rare in academic philosophy – is one small indicator of the way in which he understands how good presentation matters.

Vardy's active academic life has seen him become president of the London Society for the Study of Religions as well as a founder member of the British Society for Philosophy of Religion.

Now he is vice-principal of Heythrop College, a mostly theological college of the University of London. He is best known for his popular introductions to the philosophy of religion, which have been translated into several languages. Ironically, though one of these, *The Puzzle of God*, is compelled to trot through the standard arguments for the existence of God, Vardy has little time for them.

'I think they're a waste of time,' he says. 'I think they're boring. As a philosopher I'm interested in them. I'm interested in new revisions, I think the ontological argument particularly is fascinating. It's a lovely thing, particularly with what somebody like Norman Malcolm does with it. But I actually think they're boring because I don't think religion rests on them. You do not get someone saying, "well, I thought there was a 68 per cent chance that God exists but I've just read an article in *The Philosophers' Magazine* which has increased the probability to 71 per cent so I'm off to be a Jesuit". That's ludicrous. So I actually think they're uninteresting.'

Not only uninteresting, but misunderstood. Take, for example, Aquinas' Five Ways, widely understood to be attempts at proving the existence of God on purely rational grounds. However, as Vardy sees it, 'whether somebody like Aquinas was actually trying to show atheists that belief is rational, I think is debatable. I think what he was trying to do was to show everybody who believed – and after all, everybody did – that belief was rational. I'm not at all sure he would have conceived it as a stand-alone proof. If you look at how much he wrote in the *Summa Theologiae*, the amount devoted to the Five Ways is absolutely tiny, and if he actually thought everything was going to depend on that, I'm sure he would have devoted more than a couple of pages to it.'

Other theologians have attempted to offer not single-knock down proofs, but cumulative cases for the existence of God – where a series of arguments together serve as a cumulative proof. Alternatively, they give probability arguments to show whether the arguments add up to show God's existence is much more probable than not. Vardy doesn't believe these work either, but he also doesn't think we should be trying to simplistically judge whether they succeed or fail. 'It's not black and white,' he explains. 'Clearly they're not going to conclusively prove God exists. I think the more interesting question is, do they make it more persuasive that God does exist?

'Now my problem with that is that so much depends on what your presuppositions are. So Swinburne is going to say, put them all together and it seems probable, Flew is going to talk of leaky buckets, and I really think a lot depends on your presuppositions. Success and failure have got to be measured, not in terms of "yes it does" or "no it doesn't", but "does it increase the probability?"'

Many religious people who turn away from natural theology's attempts to provide rational grounds for belief turn to fideism – the idea that faith alone justifies belief, and faith is independent of reason.

'It's appealing,' admits Vardy, 'in that you don't have to justify your framework. You're operating within a framework and as a religious believer you know your framework is right. So if I'm a devout Muslim, I know that the Holy Koran was dictated by Allah and this is unquestioned. Can I prove it? Of course not. I can use reason within that framework. If I'm a devout Christian, I know Jesus is the second person of the trinity and rose from the dead, and I can do my reasoning within that framework.

'On the other hand, appeal to revelation can be seen, I think, philosophically as a cop-out, because which revelation do you choose? Even within Christianity there are different theories about what's revealed. Some people say through the Church – you find that more in the Catholic tradition; some people say by reading the Bible, or directly. Which revelation do we go for?'

Fideism's more sophisticated contemporary ancestor is reformed epistemology. As Vardy describes it, this is the view that 'we're justified in holding our beliefs as unjustified, because we have a properly ordered "noetic structure". That means we have been given the grace to see the world correctly. We refuse to give in to you philosophers because that would precisely be to assume that reason can judge God. We rely on revelation and we see the world correctly, we will therefore not try to reason with you – that would be natural theology. Instead we'll pray for you and you may be given the grace of God.'

Reformed epistemology has some heavyweight advocates, such as Alvin Plantinga. Once again, however, Vardy himself is not persuaded. 'I don't think that gets us anywhere. Which revelation do we go for? All this is really saying I know that I'm right in a loud voice.'

It is, however, different from fideism in one important respect. 'Somebody like Alvin Plantinga accepts the possibility of what he calls defeaters. By that he means that it is possible that within the structure of faith, that structure could be shown to be inconsistent. If therefore you could produce arguments that would show the whole structure to be incoherent, he would say we would reject it. Now defeaters can be defeated. So a defeater would be the problem of evil and that can be defeated by a theodicy, but unlike fideism, he is accepting within the structure the possibility of its being shown to be incoherent.'

The real problem Vardy has with this view is that 'if you are within the system of belief, you will be able to show people why it is reasonable not to have any justification, but somebody from outside the system is just going to simply reject your presuppositions. I think if you look at a reformed epistemologist, you can apply their argument just as much to any of the other world religions as you can to theirs. So why go for one rather than the other?'

Vardy also has a lot of respect for non-realists such as Don Cupitt who retain a religious belief while rejecting the literal existence of God, heaven and the afterlife. Vardy particularly appreciates their debt to Wittgenstein. Wittgenstein argued that the meaning of words is determined by their use in the language-using community. This brute summary does no justice to the complexity of Wittgenstein's position. However, from this basic premise it can be seen how some anti-realists have tried to defend religion along Wittgensteinian lines. They say that you can only really understand what religious language means if you are part of the religious community which uses it. To judge religious utterances from a non-religious standpoint is therefore to miss the point. That includes judging claims about God as though they referred to an entity of the same order as persons, trees or planets.

'Wittgenstein sees the complexity and sophistication of religious utterances,' explains Vardy. 'So, for instance, when he criticizes Frazer's *The Golden Bough*, Frazer is using Western anthropology to look at African religions and be pretty patronizing about it. Wittgenstein says you don't begin to understand the sophistication of this form of life. Wittgenstein wouldn't dream of judging what they're really doing, except by understanding what's happening. So take a Catholic who comes along and says, "This is the blood of Christ". For somebody to rush off and say, "well I've just analysed it in the laboratory and it's not", Wittgenstein says "for a blunder that's too big". It's stupid. What Wittgenstein I think would do would be to seek to understand how religious grammar works and then leave it at that.'

Some non-realists, however, draw the conclusion that religion is nothing more than a construct of language. Worlds are created by language users, but these worlds have no real, objective existence. So words such as 'God' and 'afterlife' do not refer to anything at all. The reason Vardy thinks this is a mistake is that 'Wittgenstein thought that philosophy should leave everything as it is. That is not what non-realists do. Non-realists are effectively saying, if it cannot be shown to be true, demonstrably (which is almost a verificationist, positivist assumption) then it's only grammar. Now that "only grammar" is not Wittgensteinian. The non-realist believes in God, believes God really really, truly truly, exists. But what they mean by existence is radically different, because they're operating with a coherence theory of truth whereby truth is dependent on your framework. Within the framework of belief, God exists.'

One reason why Vardy has some sympathy with this view is that the arguments are closer to his own interests in truth and meaning.

'The key issue, I think, today is what it means to talk about God. It used to be so simple. Fifty years ago, somebody believes in God, somebody doesn't. That's the sort of debate that Flew or Russell was involved in and in a way that's passé now. The issue is, what do you mean by God? If you talk to a non-realist, one thing that's clear is that there are ways of understanding how God exists that don't involve reference to some being called "God".'

Although he keeps it well hidden in most of his books, Vardy is not a casual commentator. He has his own beliefs and they are far from purely academic. From what he had said and written about God, I sensed he was some kind of realist – for him God exists as a real, independent entity of some kind. So why the caginess?

'I tend to be very careful about expressing where I'm coming from,' he explained, 'because I think that if one's a realist, one could be wrong and I think humility is very important. I don't think there are any conclusive arguments that can prove God exists and therefore if I stake my life on it, I could be mistaken. Therefore to try to come over to convince people with a spurious certainty when I could be mistaken I think is crazy.

'When you say I don't agree with the non-realists, I don't, but they could be right. That's why I think they should be taken seriously. I'm enough of a philosopher to think that any position that I come up with might be wrong. But one isn't a philosopher all one's life, one has to stake one's life and I think at the end of the day religion is about what you stake your life on. That isn't necessarily a matter of philosophic proof.

'I think what Christianity is about is living in a relationship with this ultimate which one calls God and trying to live that out truthfully in the world about us. Creeds, doctrines in a way are secondary. It's not a matter of saying I've got this credal formulation right, it's got much more to do with the way we live.'

Vardy talks about Karl Rahner's conception of God as Holy Mystery, 'an other which one can be in relationship with and that is not an other we construct. It is an other to whom we are accountable and responsible, on whom we depend.' Vardy believes non-realists who deny this are missing something. 'There is a sense, particularly maybe when one's in crisis, in prayer, in terms of religious experience, in terms of the possibility of life after death, in the death camps, of being in relationship with an other, being loved by this other – forgive me, it's not a philosophic term – being in the hands, if you like, of something greater which is important to the religious quest.'

His phrase 'it's not a philosophic term' is telling. Though he may reject fideism and reformed epistemology, Vardy shares with both a conviction which is beyond proof. Of his conviction that this other exists, he says, 'I can't justify it philosophically. Can I prove it? No. Can I show it to be probable? No, not at all.'

Given that he is committed to the view that philosophy of religion cannot establish religious truth, and can't even increase the probability of religious truth, what role remains for the philosophy of religion?

'I think what it's doing,' he replies, 'is first of all to provide space in a society where the whole idea of God is dismissed, that it is a serious possibility, that it can be taken seriously by sane intelligent people who are willing to think critically. A lot of people think it's off with the fairies. So that's quite important.

'Secondly, to do some critical analysis, so that you can actually follow an argument through. If you've got a particular type of God, what consequences is that going to have for religious experience, prayer, miracle, etc. You can't start defending the principle of non-contradiction – you start talking nonsense. So if you're going to say this you can't say that. So if you're going to work out a position, there might be things you can't justify, but don't bring in fifteen things you can't justify before breakfast. Actually identify what your presuppositions are.'

This could sound as much like theology as philosophy. Isn't the difference between theology and philosophy of religion that the former works within the framework of existing belief while the latter does not?

'I think that's fair,' he agrees. 'I think theology is the exploration of the framework from within and philosophy of religion is much more looking at the whole framework from without, and saying, why this framework? How does this framework work? So a philosopher of religion can look at theology and say, fine, but why operate within that framework? Why are you reading those books? Maybe the whole framework is mistaken? It's a broader view. It's standing back a bit.'

Yet since Vardy is committed to the view that philosophy cannot establish the truth or even the probability of any particular religious framework, isn't the philosophy of religion redundant? Vardy disagrees. 'There's a huge amount for it to do. A lot of theology is badly confused because they haven't done any philosophy. One of the good things about the Catholic tradition is that they actually take philosophy and theology seriously at the same time. But if you don't you end up saying a remarkable amount of nonsense. A lot of theology books, if you're not careful, use this word "God" without being at all clear what they mean by it. For instance, they'll talk about life after death and you'll get every single sort of thing you can imagine coming in. You'll get talk of souls coming in and resurrection on the last day coming in, and bodily resurrection coming in – they haven't done any philosophy. So I think philosophy needs to critique theology and to say, "what is it you are actually saying?" It also needs to push religious believers to be a lot clearer about what they're saying and I think that's an important role and it can be threatening. A lot of religious believers can be very threatened by philosophy because suddenly they have to think and that's uncomfortable.'

Vardy also clearly thinks the philosophy of religion is of use to a wider audience. He explains why by reference to his favourite philosopher – Pooh Bear.

'I think that Pooh has a wisdom and a gentleness which I would love to aspire to, and I think there's a danger of philosophy being clever. If philosophy is going to be doing anything, it's got to appeal and be able to be understandable to ordinary human beings. What I try to do in the *Puzzle* books is to set out fairly and I hope accurately different positions. I try to keep my own position in the background because that's not what matters. What I want people to do is engage with this. They must stake their own lives, so I am trying to reflect a variety of different positions. The Pooh Bears of this world are important and I would prefer to be a Pooh Bear than an Owl.'

Selected Bibliography

The Puzzle of Evil (London: Fount, 1992)
The Puzzle of Sex (London: Fount, 1997)
The Puzzle of God, rev. edn (London: Fount, 1999)
The Puzzle of Ethics, with Paul Grosch (London: Fount, 1999)
What is Truth? (Sydney: University of New South Wales, 1999)

IV Philosophy and Society

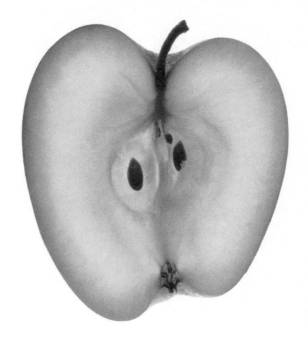

12 Murdoch and Morality

Mary Midgley

Mary Midgley has had an extraordinary career. She started with a bit of luck, being born at the right time so as to be at Oxford during the Second World War. With their male peers conscripted or volunteering to help the war effort, this gave women philosophers a real chance to make their mark in a male-dominated world. Many took it, including Midgley, Elizabeth Anscombe, Phillippa Foot and Iris Murdoch.

Midgley rose to become senior lecturer in philosophy at the University of Newcastle. Over the course of her career she has published numerous books, all characterized by their accessible style. Midgley writes philosophy that non-philosophers can understand. She also writes about topics that interest the wider public, most notably the role of science in human understanding.

The major theme that runs through Midgley's work is the idea that science, despite being one of humanity's undoubted successes, does not provide a form of knowledge that can explain or justify all spheres of human existence. Her concern has been to criticize not science, but those who make exaggerated claims for its power. She wants to keep science in its place, rather than attack it.

Her main enemy is reductionism: any view that attempts to explain human behaviour, nature or ethics in terms of simpler, more basic facts about science – usually in the form of biology, evolution or genetics. Her campaign against reductionism has been the occasion of some impassioned and high-profile debates. Most notably, she was involved in an exchange of articles with Richard Dawkins in the prestigious journal *Philosophy*. This debate was unusually impassioned and, at times, personal in nature.

All this began sixty years ago, when two young women who would go on to be among the best-known philosophers of their generation first crossed paths in Oxford. In 2000, one of the two, Dame Iris Murdoch, died of Alzheimer's disease. The following year, Mary Midgley was back in Oxford and remembering her dear departed friend.

'We both went up to Somerville in 1938,' recalls Midgley. 'We were the only two people taking our subject (Greats) in our year, so we were working together all through and we became very close. We remained close, she was a bridesmaid at my wedding. Then for a long time I was at Newcastle and I didn't see so much of her, but I always used to come and see her when I could. She's one of my closest friends and we really did grow up arguing together so much that it's a bit hard to say who was influencing who.'

The philosophies of Murdoch and Midgley parallel each other in many ways. Most obviously, both reacted strongly against the dominant 'Oxford' tradition, with its emphasis on dry linguistic analysis and its deliberate removal from everyday life. None of this would likely have occurred, however, but for the intervention of the Second World War.

'We started to do philosophy in the War, at which time all the people you think of as the Oxford philosophers, like Ryle and Ayer and so forth, were doing code and cipher at Bletchley or being dropped into European countries. A. J. Ayer's *Language, Truth and Logic* had already been published, so logical positivism was on the table. My tutor was Donald McKinnon, who was a big-time metaphysician. He was as much a theologian as a philosopher and Kant was the central theme with him. He was an old-fashioned philosopher. Both Iris and I took to that like ducks to water. Had we been presented only with the diet of narrow linguistic philosophy, I think both of us would have dropped out of it. It wasn't our kind of thing at all. We, of course, had to take note of it, and write essays on *Language, Truth and Logic* and so forth, but we both remained dedicated to the thought that philosophy was to be read as widely as possible.'

The War not only temporarily suspended the dominance of Oxford philosophy, it also opened the door to women. 'Very few people were taking Greats at all, particularly very few men. There were as many women taking it as men, so the possibility of getting one's mouth open and speaking about what interested one was much higher than usual, and I think that the fact that not only Iris and I but Elizabeth Anscombe and Phillippa Foot came out of that generation is no accident. All of us then proceeded to do what we could about stopping the narrow kind of moral philosophy that went on.

'It wasn't that we didn't get the critical analytic stuff. We did, and when we were graduate students after the War it had all come back. But at that point, the people present had come back from the War, some of them with serious injuries, and were old enough to take it or leave it. There were a lot of interesting philosophers like Strawson who came out of that generation.'

For anyone who believes that gender is a key influence on how philosophy is done, this is grist to their mill. The men go off to war and while they're away a different style of philosophy flourishes. Many women of this generation went on to specialize in what is now called 'applied philosophy', in other words, relating philosophical concerns, particularly in ethics, to real life. Does Midgley think that the fact that these philosophers were women was an important factor here?

'I do think that women are less likely to be prepared to spend their time playing games in philosophy, and that's what I think a great deal of philosophy is doing. Some of it, obviously, is simply complicated, but it's pretty far from life. I don't think that women can't perform these formal operations, but they wish to be shown some reason why they should. That's certainly my situation – I can't speak for women in general. If you're doing philosophy at all, if you're engaged in the way that ideas work, then it's a largely male peculiarity to wish to go right up in the air and go round in circles without relating them to anything else.'

A key characteristic of both Midgley's and Murdoch's reactions against the dominant Anglo-Saxon tradition has been their stress on holistic rather than reductive explanations. Midgley believes that twentieth-century philosophy worked too exclusively by breaking down and dividing up the phenomena it attempted to explain. Indeed, this is what is often understood by the notion of analysis in analytic philosophy. The cost of this, thinks Midgley, has been a failure to attend to the ways in which parts form wholes and an unrealistic world-view which sees everything as mere composites of simpler, discrete units.

'I think that Iris and I share the thought that it's terribly important to see the whole and that one is usually deceiving oneself if one says X is only Y. Sometimes there's good reason to attend only to Y. But the illusion that particular scholars tend to have is that their subject has explained everything completely.

'Iris had a Marxist angle which I think was in many ways very useful because Marxism is very wide. It's sometimes reductive itself, but it never lets you think that you've only got one side to look at. I've a slightly different angle in that I got very interested quite early in the dismissive way in which people talk about animals and the over-reductiveness of that; and in Descartes' notion that animals are not conscious because they are only machines.'

One example of this scepticism about reduction regards the traditional divide between feeling and reason. Midgley argues that one cannot divide up the mind so neatly.

'This is a complaint about something that goes much further back than Oxford analytic philosophy. From Descartes, the Enlightenment philosophizing tradition has divided feeling from reason, and has, on the whole, been shouting on the side of reason. The image, for instance, in Plato of the rider (reason) taming the horse (emotion), or of the colonial governor managing the natives has been influential.

What one wants to say is that when somebody is puzzled or distressed by something, for example, they are doing one large thing of which feeling and reason are two aspects.'

Again, it is curious that the loudest voices calling for such holistic approaches have been those of women, but Midgley does not believe this opens the door to a view of philosophy as essentially gendered, because, as she says, 'I want to say that we are all both. I do think very profoundly that we are all male and all female, that these are elements in all of us, that there should not be and isn't warfare. You can find holistic male philosophers – Aristotle certainly was, and Butler, and I think on their good days people like Plato are both. The trouble is that with their disciples and the formation of schools, these things always get more extreme.'

So though men and women in philosophy tend to pull in different directions, it's not a matter of a fundamental divide, but rather one of a shift of emphasis. But philosophy needs both typically male and female influences in order for it to be done best. This is as true for the systems and cultures of universities as it is for arguments and theories.

'The thing I complain of in universities is that you get great numbers of young men who have to make their way. Inevitably things are competitive. The business of winning arguments becomes very important, the lawyerly side of philosophizing is bound to come out. I think it is true that if you have some more women around less of this happens. If you had it the other way on planet X and mostly the women were doing it, it is quite likely that they wouldn't be coming off the fence enough.'

Another division both Murdoch and Midgley are keen to dispute is the long-cherished distinction between facts and values. It has become something of a truism in philosophy that one cannot derive truths about values, particularly moral values, from value-free facts about the world. Murdoch tried to undermine this idea through her notion of attending. How does Midgley understand this idea?

'We are always treating people in ways which we think are appropriate to them *as we see them* – we think we've got the facts about these people. If we attend more closely we may often realize that these were not the relevant facts, the facts are more complicated. This is all a way of getting away from the simple fact/value dichotomy which was what we were all fighting in the early days, and it's still there. One's business is not only to respond to the situation in which one finds oneself, but also to make sure that one knows what the situation is, by attending.

'[Murdoch's] *The Sovereignty of Good* is really a book about freedom. Iris is attacking the view that what we have to do is primarily to be free, that our duty is to act and that there isn't really any value or importance in our states of mind and the inner life doesn't matter. This is, as she says, really an existentialist position. She says your inner life is actually really important, because you have an attitude, a way of thinking about, and a way of seeing the things and people that you're involved with, and it is your business to see whether that way of seeing is realistic. If you simply put your moral effort into making up your own mind and acting freely but don't attend to what's happening you're very obviously missing out on a lot of what really matters.'

So on Murdoch's view of ethics, we learn what is the right thing to do, the good, by attending to what is the case and increasing our understanding of reality. That's why she thinks art is important, because art increases our sense of reality. The fact/value distinction is dissolved because if you had a full appreciation of reality you would come to know what is the right thing.

Another striking similarity between the philosophy of Murdoch and Midgley is that they both stress how important it is to think of the myths and metaphors we use, most particularly when we fail to realize that we are speaking metaphorically.

'What people take to be proper, official thinking is often a pared-down version of a myth and metaphor that they've been using, such as the selfish gene and viewing people as machines. It is extraordinary, I think, how many theorists seem not to know when they are using a metaphor. "The human mind just is a computer made of meat," for example. And when Dawkins quotes Nick Humphrey saying about memes, "when you give me your idea you literally parasitize my mind," it's not just that people are using metaphors of which they are not totally aware but they use these metaphors explicitly as facts.'

Analytic philosophers won't warm to this theme, because metaphors represent ambiguity and ambivalence, whereas analytic philosophers see themselves as giving clear, unambiguous explanations. Metaphor is therefore a threat to objective truth. Midgley would have it the other way around. By accepting and by being fully aware of the element of metaphor in what you're saying, you see the broader picture and the truth of what you're saying more clearly.

'If they delude themselves that they're doing without metaphors they are likely to be mistaken. We're always using them and I think that a lot of apparently reductive and rigorous thought is distorted because it's still containing metaphors. It just hasn't noticed.'

The issue of metaphor is interesting, because recently Midgley has been working with the idea of Gaia, which she has sympathy with – the idea that the earth as a whole can be understood as a single, living organism. Isn't this no more than a metaphor?

'You say "no more than a metaphor", but that is something absolutely enormous. If, on the one hand, you ask for the literal translation then you get an awful lot of science, which they're all busy on. On the other hand you get a way of viewing things, an imaginative framework within which you see the world differently and on seeing it differently you also feel differently towards it. If indeed this story is true as it appears to be, that life, all the life on the living earth, has succeeded in keeping the conditions liveable on this planet for nearly as long as the planet has been around, contrary to all kinds of trends which would otherwise have taken place, then the only possible response is one of awe and gratitude. If you notice that you're using a metaphor, the response it not usually, "oh well, I only meant ..." but "let's unpack what is involved in this".'

Iris Murdoch herself was modest about her achievements in philosophy. 'She wouldn't consider herself as contributing at all, which is a great pity,' claims Midgley. Her reputation as a novelist is far greater than her reputation as a philosopher. Nevertheless, Midgley does believe Murdoch has made a vital contribution to the subject.

'I think that putting the inner life back is a frightfully important thing. The behaviouristic element in the Hare and Hampshire line was terrible and they were quite unaware that it was so. They felt, with a certain sense of righteousness, that people ought only to be concerned with actions. "We wouldn't indulge in attending to states of minds, this would be Epicurean, too self-centred, too irresponsible." Well, I think the inner life is absolutely essential to our power of action. We couldn't possibly do without it. The unhappiness and distress that a lot of people are in now is due to not realizing this.'

Selected Bibliography

Beast and Man: The Roots of Human Nature (London: Methuen, 1980)

Wickedness: A Philosophical Essay (London: Routledge, 1984)

Science as a Salvation (London: Routledge, 1992)

The Ethical Primate (London: Routledge, 1994)

Science and Poetry (London: Routledge, 2001)

13 Justice and Conflict

Stuart Hampshire

Stuart Hampshire is one of the leading philosophers of his generation. Born as the First World War was starting, his philosophical career took a break while he served in the army during the Second, followed by a stint at the Foreign Office. Once he resumed philosophy his trajectory was onwards and upwards. He became the Grote Professor of Mind and Logic at University College London in 1960, then held professorships at Princeton and Stanford universities in the USA. He also served as warden of Wadham College, Oxford.

Hampshire became best known for his work on issues of human free will and the relationship between thought and action. Many students will know him for his book on Spinoza, which, since its publication in 1951, many still consider an unsurpassed introduction to the subject. In recent years, however, he has become increasingly concerned with political philosophy, and has published, at the age of 85, a lucid and fresh work on the subject: *Justice Is Conflict*.

The book contains several ideas. First, it accepts as a basic premise that matters of fundamental value cannot be settled by reasoning alone. So, for example, the conviction – which Hampshire shares – that poverty is a great evil, the eradication of which should be the prime goal of politics, cannot be shown, on purely rational grounds, to be superior to the conviction that extending freedom should be the main goal of politics. Which side you come down on is a matter of conviction, not logic.

But although values are pluralistic in this sense, Hampshire believes there is something in politics which has a claim to universality. That is, it is a demand of reason that when goals or values come into conflict – which they inevitably will – the conflict should be resolved not by force or coercion, but by a rational, deliberative process of 'hearing both sides'. Hampshire thus makes the requirement for mechanisms through which to hear both sides fairly, a universal demand on all political systems and on adherents of opposing political convictions.

When we spoke, it was about Hampshire's recent political work. A strong theme which comes through in *Justice Is Conflict* is the idea that political thought is no longer guided by the positive vision of what an ideal society should be like. Hampshire argues that, instead, we should focus on the negative vision, on what's wrong with society and try to remedy that.

'The argument runs like this,' says Hamshire. 'Individuals find themselves divided in their desires and ambitions, they have every kind of ambivalence and so forth. Plato has an idea that society reflects the conflicts which are in the soul – or different parts of the soul, as he puts it. Ordinarily this notion is dismissed by commentators as just a mistake, but I think it isn't a mistake and it's unavoidable given the fact that we constantly change our desires, our targets, and what we attach value to, for all sorts of complex reasons. If we had fixed natures we would be more like the animals than we are. And hence we cannot suppose that we can get people together, as John Rawls supposes, to agree on a minimum set of values which we can all subscribe to. The different ideals which people have – military ideals, priest-like ideals, commercial ideals and so forth – the different kinds of life which people want to pursue are irreducibly plural. Hence we have to shift from looking for what unites us to procedures which are used to moderate and negotiate disagreements.

'Consider also our own deliberations, where we have to arbitrate between something which we think we ought to do as part of our profession, and something that we want to do as part of our private life. We have to have some method – which we call deliberation, a term that really comes out of Aristotle's *Nicomachean Ethics* more than anything – of balancing these. Although there is no formula which tells us what to do, there is something which we call rational procedure, which Aristotle describes as weighing two sides – in this case, the claims which our private life makes and the claims which our public life makes.

'This is really derivative from public procedures which all societies have. We reflect from the public procedures back on to the private procedures, not the other way. It never could be the case that we should set up a rational method of solving our conflicts, as it were, *de novo*, if we didn't have the procedures or processes that go on in the state, when it has to decide whether to go to war or not, for example.'

Although Hampshire's view of values is pluralistic, it is interesting that the one value which remains universal is this deliberative process. What is Hampshire's reply to the critic who asks why it is privileged, why it is the only value which is allowed universality?

'Because we can't avoid it,' he replies. 'For example, it is necessary that you should have a conflict between, let's take a banal case, your responsibilities as a teacher or professor and your responsibilities as a husband, wife or father. They come into conflict. Or you get a conflict between your desire to have an academic life, but also to have a reasonable income. You can't have both. Then you have to weigh them. It is not simply a matter of morality, you still have to weigh in matters of prudence.'

Although such conflicts may be inevitable, the requirement to weigh both sides is easily avoided by somebody who just says, 'I'm not going to listen to both sides. In my own case, I must have to, but politically I'm basically going to force through my own view.'

'Your point that one cannot say that the value of rationality which governs your deliberations about your own dilemmas is unavoidable is absolutely valid,' admits Hampshire. 'It's unavoidable that people know rationality exists. They might be able to dismiss its claims in public life and say, "I'm going for broke and I'm simply going to pursue my own interests and pay no interest to anybody else". That is certainly so. I'm not producing a transcendental deduction, in Kant's phrase, that everybody *must* observe this. This would be to prove too much, because it's quite evidently the case that you may pursue your ends by domination. There is a genuine choice in public life between following the rational method, whether or not it's a democratic method, or not. The deduction is only that you must accept that there is a difference between settling a dispute by rationality and settling it by force.'

So is the preference for settling it by rationality a basic value which cannot itself be argued for?

'Yes. There is one argument for it which is derived from what we do when we consider nobody except ourselves. It's perfectly intelligible to claim universality for it by pointing to how people proceed in their own case. When they have to balance two or more targets that they have, they do proceed by seeing the pros and cons.'

Political philosophy is often far removed from the reality of political life. How far does Hampshire think that the kind of post-ideological socialism being implemented by people like the British Prime Minister Tony Blair is in tune with his vision for politics?

'I don't think that Blair is at all in tune with me. I think his rhetoric presupposes that the class war is dead, which may be true if you stress the word "class", but the conflict of interests between the rich and the poor is, I think, still very significant. But he tries to argue, and I think a lot of people agree with him, that there is a supernational purpose which the economic system can serve, which means that the worker and the manager have the same interests and there is no necessary conflict. I think – though this point is perhaps more for economics than mere philosophy – that there is still the same conflict. If you are selling your labour you want to sell it as high as you can go and if you are buying it you want to buy it cheap, and it's no good saying this isn't a conflict. It certainly is.

'They're pretending that conflicts arise out of some stupidity or lack of perception of the persons involved. The rhetoric cuts across a great deal of traditional economics. There is an argument of a highly technical kind to be held here as to whether this vision, which was very dominant just after the War, that if the trade unions sit down with the managers, they can all agree on a policy which will satisfy all their needs or demands, is correct. I believe that is an untrue picture of how the economy works. But you've got to argue that.

'The actual situation is that if you have the proper institutions for settling wages and conditions of work, you get them by fighting for them and that's how the workers have got them. If they get deceived and stop standing up for their own needs, they'll lose what they've gained.

'It's a question of how you view the way the economy works. It's implied by the Blair people that this feature of late capitalism, that the rich get enormously richer and the poor either remain static or get positively poorer, is somehow very surprising and to be dealt with by minor measures of patching it up. But I think it lies in the nature of capitalism that this will happen.'

The pluralistic element in Hampshire's position is very strong. Although he thinks that it is a universal idea that we have the proper procedures and institutions to deal with conflicts, he allows that within such institutions, which we can all accept, things may be permitted which we may personally, from a moral viewpoint, find repugnant. Hampshire gives the example of the immigration laws: he strongly disagrees with them but he respects the institutions which gave rise to them. But what happens when the systems allow something which we find very strongly morally repugnant? The claim of justice on us is that we respect the institutions that balance the competing interests, but the deeper moral commitments we have would sometimes seem to come into conflict with that.

'Of course, I'm not saying that justice, which for me is a matter of obeying the procedurally accepted method, overrides all other values,' says Hampshire. 'On the contrary, there do arise situations

where you have to say there are other values. Removing extreme
cruelty, for example, overrides the demands of justice. It is in the
nature of morals, I think, that you have conflicts and that you can't
say that one virtue overrides all other virtues no matter what.'

But if there can be conflicts between justice and other moral
values, in what sense does the justice component remain universal?
To be universal but not without exception might be thought to
amount to not being universal at all.

'If you have a dispute between two different virtues or values,
then you have to have some way of thinking about it which
arbitrates between them. You know very well that in a difficult case
you may later think that you're wrong and other people may think
that you're wrong. There is no sense of definitively proving
something, but there is a case of going about it in a methodical
and rational way. I think that's all one can say.'

Hampshire's view sounds like good common sense, but although
philosophers who are still attached to the universalizing, system-
atizing impulse could go along with Hampshire up to a point, what
they would want to do then is try to discover a system that perfectly
deals with the need to balance both sides. Why does Hampshire
think that any attempt to come up with a single system would be
doomed?

'The orthodox answer, which I don't stress, is that because the
social conditions so totally change with changing technologies, a
kind of quasi-Marxist way of looking at it, these old systems are just
inapplicable. Blair has a point with this otherwise empty, it seems to
me, notion of "modernization". It's true that if the social structure
changes in such a way that people can communicate on the web
and transact their affairs in a totally different way then you have to
change the procedures, for example, over libel. That is the orthodox
answer, and there are certain things parliament can't do any more
because they happen too fast and parliament can't control them.

'But I think there's a more profound factor than this and that is
that people's ideals change. The old feudal ideals of the warrior – of

honour and martial virtues and loyalty no matter what – these were prevailing ideals which no longer have any hold over people. What we regard as a desirable life changes and we get tempted away in different directions.

'So there is that element of mutability and I think the mutability of human nature is much the most important feature of it.'

One way in which Hampshire suggests his ideas could cash out practically is that 'bringing into existence institutions and recognized procedures should have priority over declarations of universal principles'.

'I say that to counter the American political tradition, which is of course one of declaring certain principles, building them into the constitution, and then having the constitution protected by a body of lawyers. I don't think that international institutions can be set up in that way. They can only be set up by the acquisition of the habit of going to certain kinds of institution, such as an international court. But if you merely lay down principles, they don't grip. They only grip if you have a body of people who work together in a certain way across frontiers.'

Hampshire describes himself as a socialist, but a lot of what he says would suggest that the real victor ideologically has been liberalism. Would Hampshire accept that he is as much a liberal as a socialist?

'It's too loose a word,' he counters. 'A lot of what I said could be said by someone living in a Greek city-state, rather than by a nineteenth-century liberal. If I mention the word "socialism", I give it a sense by saying a socialist is somebody who wants to extend the domain of human interest which the state regards itself responsible for. It doesn't say that poverty just arises, rather that it arises from a natural process of how the economy works and that there should be a gradual extension of state power to remedy what are generally agreed to be evils. That's all I mean by socialism. If somebody says that's fairly abstract I have to admit it is. I'm arguing at an abstract level. The ways that socialists have so far tried to make that effective on the ground have not themselves been very effective, that has to be admitted. State socialism of the orthodox kind has been an obvious failure. But one might still hold that it is the duty of institutions in Britain or wherever to do what they can, and find out what they can, to mitigate the obvious evils. That's the only sense of socialism.

'If you ask, "has liberalism triumphed?" I don't think so. I think that liberals are a small section in Britain, America, Canada and Australia. Fortunately, they have superior access to power.'

But surely there is a sense in which liberalism has triumphed, in that, for example, people defending socialism now are defending it within a liberal framework.

'That's true,' accepts Hampshire. 'I'm defending it in a liberal framework, in the American sense of liberal. I'm not saying anything of the Leninist kind, that you must subordinate any principle of justice to achieve some end.'

Hampshire's thesis in many ways humbles political philosophy, in that it robs it of the idea that it can be the great constructor. But there's one way in which it puts political philosophy centre-stage again, which is that he returns to the Platonic model that the understanding of the State and the individual go together. What brought him back to that?

'I have a very strong feeling that we have to define what the sphere or range of politics is. I think it is everything that is disputed at a fundamental moral level. Therefore, it's irrational and positively harmful for people to regard politics just as a thing some people go in for and that it is intrinsically not very important. I suppose that might be said to be a socialist thought, that whatever is your first or second interest, your third interest, whoever you are, ought to be politics, on the grounds of rationality. If you accept rationality as a value – though I wouldn't want to make it the central value and derive everything from it, that seems to me a mistake – people who are engaged in politics are engaged in an activity which everybody ought to be interested in. I want to boost the perception of politics and dismiss the idea that if only we cleared up our minds about what is good and bad, we wouldn't need politics. On the contrary, it's the process of conflict, rightly regulated, which is the most important practical process.'

Hampshire's arguments refer obliquely to many strands in philosophy, not just political philosophy. For instance, he sees the reasoning which we undertake privately to be modelled on the public forms of decision-making, which has echoes of Gilbert Ryle's claims that a lot of things we think of as being essentially mental are public first and private second.

'It's indebted to the whole system of philosophy which Ryle's *The Concept of Mind* was part of,' he acknowledges, 'of which, I suppose, the major figure was Wittgenstein – which held that we could only learn these phrases that we have for mental processes in social exchanges. That's an independent thesis which seems to be certainly true.'

Hampshire's thesis that conflict resolution is at the heart of political justice demands a conflict resolution mechanism. The one he advocates, he describes as adversarial – seeing both sides, weighing them up. In taking that model, is Hampshire guilty of parochialism, as it just so happens that the political tradition in Britain has always been adversarial, arguably more so than in other countries?

'No,' he counters, 'because the process of adversarial law, advocacy, is universal. Wherever people are gathered into social groups, there will be adversarial reasoning going on, usually over property, status or something of that kind. People are driven to it. The question is how evolved are the adversarial processes? How much do they displace mere force?'

Hampshire's political philosophy involves some interesting claims about metaphilosophy – the nature and methods of philosophy itself. He suggests that for this process of settling conflict, we need as a model of reason, of rationality, something which stands in opposition to the idea of reason being essentially deductive along the mathematical model. However, the procedures by which he proposes we undertake this process of conflict resolution are in some sense dependent upon the kind of principles established in deductive reasoning, such as the law of non-contradiction. So how far is it true that he's advocating the replacement of this deductive model in our understanding of what reason is?

'Obviously, not in the bare outlines of logic. It's not the deduction that's important, it is that which it aims at: conclusions which nobody who follows the process can deny, what I call in the book "convergent reasoning". If you're going to ask about numbers, anyone who is competent in the subject will accept the conclusions of the theorems you arrive at. That's that. It's the essence of practical problems that it's never "that's that" in that sense. Bertrand Russell in his autobiography said that when he read Euclid he suddenly emerged into a world which he found perfect because results are proved, there's no argument. It really reduces to the claim that life's not like that. Reasoning which is really working is reasoning that can go wrong, where you take a risk. You do everything you can do to get it right, but maybe you don't get it right, or maybe it's not clear what getting it right actually is.'

These are the kinds of risks that Hampshire has taken all his career and it is the ability to take them and succeed that marks out the really good philosophers from the also-rans. Hampshire has always been in the former camp and is certainly not ready to give up his place now.

Selected Bibliography

Spinoza, rev. edn (Harmondsworth: Penguin, 1987)
Thought and Action (London: Chatto and Windus, 1959)
Morality and Conflict (Oxford: Blackwell, 1983)
Freedom of the Individual (London: Chatto and Windus, 1965)
Justice Is Conflict (London: Duckworth, 1999)

14 Art's Value

Roger Scruton

Roger Scruton admits to being what many people would call an elitist. He thinks that some tastes are better than others. Specifically, he has a preference for high culture over popular culture and believes that this preference can be rationally grounded. Of course, probably everybody agrees that art, literature and music – the things that make up both high and popular culture – have value. Their centrality in human life, and the pleasure that they bring, make denying this proposition almost an absurdity. However, the idea that some art has more value than other art is contentious. It isn't immediately clear what could ground such a difference. In his writings, Scruton suggests that part of the story is that high art functions to transform our lives, ridding them of their arbitrariness and contingency. I ask him how this might occur.

'I take it that there is a real question about what constitutes the value of high art,' he responds. 'It requires a lot of thinking and discipline to appreciate and to understand. We are living in a period when many people do not see the point of making the effort required for understanding difficult works of art, so unless you can say something about what you gain from them, the whole enterprise is jeopardized.

'Now, human ambitions are necessarily compromised; our lives cannot be so constructed that they move of their own accord to a satisfying conclusion; they cannot be constructed so that each part casts light on another part and seems fully satisfied by that other part. Our goals are frustrated. Our lives fall to pieces. Nothing seems to come to fruition. And this is all inevitable because of the empirical circumstances in which we live.

'Nevertheless, it is part of being human that our ambitions and loves are framed according to our ideals: not just things that we want, but things that it would be right to want, and that would fulfil us were we to obtain them. The ideal is not attainable in reality, but we imagine what it would be like to attain it, when we see it fully realized in the imaginative work of art. This applies even when the realization involves the destruction of a character, as in tragedy. Tragedy vindicates the ideal, by showing people how to be greater, more interesting, more worthy of praise, than the forces that destroy them. Contemplating tragedy, our lives are illuminated by the meaning that we see.'

In this sense, it seems that for Scruton high art is a moral phenomenon through and through. I ask him whether it is his view that the ethical life can only be sustained and renewed through the work of the imagination.

'I don't want to say that it is only through art or the imagination that you can live an ethical life,' he replies. 'The best art is devoted to the task of making the ethical life worthwhile, and showing that all the costs involved in it are fully compensated. That is something that you find in Shakespeare's great tragedies. Although there is a huge cost involved in thinking in terms of right and wrong, duty and virtue, and living in this way – living in the eyes of judgement – there is also the greatest of benefits. Judgement raises us to the level where fulfilment is possible. So art and imagination offer us light in the darkness. But this doesn't mean that people who have no feeling for art cannot live decent lives. On the contrary, of course they can.'

It is also true that art can be involved in people living very unethical lives. The example of Hitler and his love of Wagner springs to mind.

'People always give this example,' admits Scruton. 'You cannot say that works of art will always have a good effect on people, even if their moral content is of the highest order. What effect they have depends upon the kind of person we're talking about. An evil person will gain sustenance from a great work of art. But I think it is nonsense to suppose that this necessarily tells you anything about the work of art itself. Anything that had an effect on Hitler was going to have a bad effect, just as any water poured into a poisoned drain will come out poisoned.'

The problem with this reply is just that there are people who don't agree. They think that there *is* something about Wagner's music which explains why it was so attractive to Hitler. So I ask whether there is any way of settling this dispute.

'Well, the specific case about Wagner *is* still very much alive. But consider that Goebbels was very much moved by Mozart. Stalin had pretty developed musical tastes. Mao Tse-tung was moved by classical Chinese poetry, some of which contains what people claim are perfect statements of the old Confucian ethic. Yet all of those people went on to commit terrible crimes. I think you have to recognize that our appreciation and understanding of works of art is in the first instance isolated from life – that's the whole point of aesthetic experience, that it enables us to contemplate life from a position of solemn detachment. Works of art are not there to influence or guide our actions. They are there to be contemplated; but from the act of contemplation we gain a sense of what is meaningful. And this feeds our moral sense.

'The fact that there are bad people moved by works of art doesn't taint those works of art; you have to think of all the good people moved by them too. And maybe the only good thing about these bad people is that they *were* moved by those great works of art.'

According to Scruton, part of the distinction between high and popular culture has to do with the way that some art objects genuinely engage the imagination as opposed to being merely objects of fantasy. I ask him what's involved in this distinction.

'Fantasy objects are substitutes,' he replies. 'They are a way of titillating real emotions and giving substitute satisfaction. The imaginative act, in contrast, is an endeavour to create a possible world, an imaginative world, where the emotions are also imaginary. So the artist is not offering a substitute satisfaction for a real emotion – art is not like pornography, for example. Rather, the artist is making someone imagine both the object and the emotion directed towards it. The artist explores an imagined world as a free being with all moral commitments engaged. That tells us the difference between, for example, the erotic and the pornographic.'

It is not at all clear, however, that it is easy to draw these kinds of distinctions. For example, thinking about the difference between erotic art and pornography, it seems possible that the same object might produce different reactions in different people. So, for some people, an art object might result in an imaginative act and for other people it might be purely an object of sexual fantasy.

'This is difficult,' admits Scruton. 'You have to think in terms of the language of literary critics. Leavis talks about works of art that invite a certain response. We know what that means, although it is difficult to specify it precisely. We know this because we know it in life. We know that there are people who invite a sentimental response to themselves, and others who remain distant, as if there is something still to be got from them. In the same way, we recognize this in art. Kitsch is a form of cheap invitation, and pornography is an invitation to fantasy sex. The erotic, in contrast, puts the sexual object at a distance – so that it becomes an object of contemplation. And the passion that erotic art arouses is an imaginative passion, not a real one. You can see this, for example, in Titian's nudes, which are very good examples of erotic art. A Titian Venus is not masturbation material at all. The whole image is veiled by contemplation and idealized. It is not a woman for the taking, but rather a woman who is thinking of her own lover. To grasp the atmosphere of the picture, you have to set it at a distance from yourself.'

Scruton draws a similar distinction between real feelings and sentimental feelings. I ask him how this cashes out in terms of an understanding of high and popular culture.

'These are very difficult philosophical questions,' he replies. 'Sentimentality is one of those things which is very hard to define. I take the line that the crucial feature of a sentimental emotion is that while it might appear that its intent is to exit outwards towards an object, it is in fact only a pretence that the object is the real focus of its concern. Its real focus is the subject. So the thought is not "how sad" about that object, but rather "how refined and touching of me to be feeling 'how sad' about that object".'

For Scruton, then, it seems that in drawing the distinction between high and popular culture, the notions of sentimentality and fantasy are central.

'Well, I wouldn't want to argue that all popular culture is kitsch,' he cautions. 'But there is truth in what people like Adorno say, that there are different levels at which we respond to art, and some responses are much easier to achieve than others. They are easier to achieve because they involve either a kind of emotional laziness or engagement with self-satisfied feelings.

'Now, there are different reasons why something might be easy to engage with. But one reason is that it is simply eliciting a stock response. The response is automatic, involving no reflection on the object. In such cases sentimentality is always in the wings. If you are just giving vent to a stock response, the thing which is most important to you is not the object, it is yourself.'

Arguably, the difficulty with this kind of argument is that it is value-laden. Surely, it is possible just to reply, well, the whole point of art is to produce a sentimental response?

'That's one come-back,' agrees Scruton, 'just to say, well what's wrong with sentimentality? I feel that one of the great achievements of English literary criticism since Coleridge is that it has not only tried to answer that question, but has actually given an account of what is wrong with sentimentality.

'Essentially, sentimentality puts a veil between you and the world. It makes your own feelings more important than their object, and thereby neutralizes the feelings. You are not really responding to the world as it is; hence there is an epistemological defect in sentimentality. Leavis brings this out very brilliantly in his analysis of the Hardy and Tennyson poems in 'Reality and Sincerity'. He succeeds in showing just how concrete the vision of the world is in Hardy, and how he is interrogating objects and using them to interrogate himself. Each detail is raising an evaluative question, not only about the thing itself, but also about the quality of the emotion directed towards it. Whereas in Tennyson, there is an easy flow of emotion, which washes over things so that you hardly see them. There is no self-interrogation, and no interrogation of the object. The level of awareness is diminished.'

There's an interesting question about what's at stake here. The talk has been about the different levels at which one can respond to art. As someone who prefers popular culture to high culture, despite having had fairly extensive exposure to the latter, I wonder whether any moral, and perhaps behavioural, consequences follow as a result of a preference for sentimentality and fantasy.

'I think there certainly are,' responds Scruton. 'This is a delicate question, because it depends upon how important artistic and cultural matters are in the life of a person. The artistic choices people make don't reveal that much if art isn't particularly important in their life. But when art becomes integrated into your life, then it does become a sign of what sort of person you are. It also becomes a means of communicating with others, which is a very important role that art plays in our culture at least. We use our artistic tastes in order to clarify our feelings about other things, not only to ourselves, but to each other. That's one of the reasons that we are *suitors for agreement*, as Kant says in the *Critique of Judgement*. The aesthetic judgement is never just "I like that, you don't"; there is always an attempt to use the aesthetic object to cast light on your own way of life.

'Thus I would find it extremely difficult to live with somebody whose main interest was pop music. Not only because I cannot stand the sound of it, but because it would mean that communication would be curtailed, and a source of judgement would be neutralized.

'On the other hand,' continues Scruton, 'I can see that this is too simple a view. There's a part of me that likes pop music too. I can read about pop music enthusiasts and get a sense of how it might be thrilling to be even the most abject kind of MTV addict. Take Salman Rushdie's novel *The Ground Beneath Her Feet*. It is about two Indian pop idols, and it conveys some of the sense – though I think a completely delusive sense – of pop as a spiritual crystallization of modernity. I can see how someone can get to the point of liking pop music for this reason, believing it to be a vivid symbol of modern life, and a means to engage in that life.'

These remarks about popular music are interesting because they are suggestive of a worry that some people might have about philosophers talking about popular culture. The worry is that they are not sufficiently immersed in the culture to be able to talk about it persuasively. I wonder whether Scruton sees this as a problem.

'Well, when I write about pop music, I write about it from a distant perspective, that's true,' admits Scruton. 'But I say things about it that a musician would say about it, rather than what an enthusiast would say. And the musical fundamentals of popular music haven't changed.'

The suspicion, though, is that in writing about popular music from a distance, it will inevitably be the most popular of pop music that will be the focus of attention. The difficulty is that this kind of pop music is not representative of the musical genre as a whole. In this regard, it is interesting that in his *An Intelligent Person's Guide to Modern Culture*, Scruton talks about pop music as being characterized by a level of harmonic impoverishment that rules out the construction of proper melodies. He also claims that many of today's popular music icons are lyrically inarticulate to such an extent that they are effectively rendered silent. There are, of course, plenty of examples of popular music where both these things are true. But equally, there are many examples where they are not, even if normally one has to look outside the 'Top 40' to find them. Why then focus on the least sophisticated kinds of popular music?

'Well, I picked those examples precisely to illustrate the phenomenon that I was talking about,' responds Scruton. 'I wasn't talking about popular music *per se*, but a particular audience for popular music, and the society-building force within it. I suppose I was generalizing from the taste of my American students at the time. But, of course, there is very sophisticated pop music. Someone like Eric Clapton has a great understanding of melodic form and harmonic progression – and also of how to make both fit together.

'I wouldn't want to condemn all popular music,' he says. 'The more it moves in the direction of proper voice-leading and harmonic understanding, the clearer the emotions, the quieter the tone, the less iconoclastic and Dionysian the result. You see that in the Beatles, and even in the Rolling Stones. What I am trying to do is to initiate a critique from within popular music – to say what is good, and what is bad, in terms that even the lover of pop can recognize.'

What seems to be at the heart of Scruton's insistence that high culture is superior to popular culture is the belief that in an important way one gains a richer experience of the world and a deeper moral understanding by involvement in it than one could by involvement in popular culture.

'The position I would like to defend,' he replies, when I put this to him, 'is one that some people would call elitist, though I don't regard that as a term of abuse. I think you can be an elitist without being a snob. You can think that some tastes are better than others, not just because they are more satisfying, but because they engage in a more creative and fulfilling way with the human soul, without condemning people who don't have those tastes. That is the position that I would like to take, because I know what the love of serious music has given to me – not just enjoyment at the sound of it, but an insight into what matters.

'I was thinking about this, this morning. As I woke up, I had the thought that the twentieth century had been full of the most wonderful farewells, and I thought of Mahler's *Das Lied von der Erde*, Strauss's *Four Last Songs*, Thomas Mann's *Dr Faustus*, and James

Joyce's *Ulysses*. Those are all incredible farewells, and I thought how wonderful it is to have known these things, and to see how to be reconciled not only to your own death, but also to the death of a civilization. I woke with a sense of gratitude that this had been given to me through art. I don't think it could have been given to me in any other way.'

Selected Bibliography

The Aesthetics of Music (London: Clarendon, 1997)
An Intelligent Person's Guide to Modern Culture (London: Duckworth, 1998)

15 Women Philosophers

Mary Warnock

Mary Warnock is probably the most famous philosopher in Britain. She was one of the generation of women philosophers for whom the Second World War provided a chance to step out of the shadows of their male peers. She became an Oxford fellow and later the Mistress of Girton College, Cambridge, but by her own reckoning she has been more of an efficient than a star philosopher. Her fame rests upon her popular writing and, more importantly, her role in public life.

Her high-profile public roles have included membership of the Independent Broadcasting Authority, chairing an enquiry into the education of children with special needs, and heading a government committee of enquiry into the ethics of human fertilization and embryology. She was made a life peer in 1985, entitling her to sit in the United Kingdom's second parliamentary chamber, one of only a few philosophers to do so.

She has also written a number of books aimed beyond the usual readership of academics and students. Her *Intelligent Person's Guide to Ethics* was well received, and she has also published a memoir and an anthology of writings by women philosophers.

Warnock thus stands out as a highly successful woman in a field which is still – at the top level at least – dominated by men. And yet mention her name among those most passionate about the need for gender equality in philosophy and you are unlikely to hear a chorus of approval.

Though she might not relish the comparison, Warnock's position mirrors that of Margaret Thatcher, the most successful woman in her field yet a pariah among most feminists. In both cases, the source of the rift is the same: both women have succeeded themselves while denying the importance of feminism in their fields. So, for example, the philosopher Beverley Clack wrote disparagingly in *The Philosophers' Magazine* that 'Warnock seems to suggest that feminism's concern with the position and experience of women is an aberration.' While such comments lack the venom which attacks on Thatcher inspire, it's hard not to conclude that for many feminists, there is a taint of betrayal about both of them.

It is not then perhaps surprising that Mary Warnock was at first reluctant to talk about women in philosophy, expressing a lack of interest in both components of the theme. However, talk she did, and her views present a reading of the place of women in philosophy which challenges much received wisdom, and which must be taken seriously. In our discussion, she disputed one by one virtually every claim made by feminist philosophers.

First of all, she disputes claims that women thinkers have been marginalized. 'I just don't think there was a great number of women philosophers who have been neglected.' Referring back to the early days of modern philosophy, in the seventeenth and eighteenth centuries, Warnock says, 'Philosophy was a peculiar subject in any case at that time. It was very much parasitic on the sciences and not very many women – well no women really – had much of a chance to do more than express an interest in the sciences and didn't have the chance, obviously, to pursue the foundations of science and look at what revolutions were going on in science in the way that men did. So I think it would be very difficult to dredge up many or any unduly neglected women philosophers. After that, philosophy began to be a professional university subject and obviously women couldn't compete for a long time in that field.' Warnock does not then deny that women have not been given the opportunities that men have historically had to excel at philosophy. She just feels that this is what explains the low number of women philosophers in the canon, not any gender-bias in the selection of that canon. Philosophy by women has not been passed over; it has just been thin on the ground.

Warnock is dismissive of *prima facie* evidence to the contrary. For example, in her anthology *Women Philosophers* there are extracts from L. Susan Stebbing and Susanne K. Langer, contemporaries of Moore and Whitehead. However, while the two men are still on undergraduate reading lists, the women are not. Is that anything to do with their gender?

'I don't think so at all,' replies Warnock. 'After all, there are dozens and dozens of male philosophers whom nobody reads any more who will probably come back again.'

While researching her anthology of women philosophers, Warnock noticed that the writing of some of the candidates for inclusion was too steeped in religious doctrine to qualify as proper philosophy. It seems to Warnock that women philosophers had found it more difficult to disentangle their philosophy from their religious beliefs. Why was that?

'I think that most women, even the cleverest of them, were locked in their traditional role of being the supportive, probably religious, members of the household who held things together, and it would have been quite shocking for many of them openly to abandon religion, although of course some of them did, but they were very bold spirits. On the whole it was more difficult for them to forget about religion.

'It was perfectly acceptable for women to write religious, pious sorts of tracts, for want of a better word. That was an acceptable way for women to publish their thoughts and feelings, and I think it was because they weren't at that early stage educated in philosophy as a separate subject that, if they had philosophical thoughts, they tended to write them up as religious. So I think that is simply a matter of history.'

Warnock's scepticism about feminism's claims is also evident in her unwillingness to portray her own career as in any way an

example of a woman fighting a male-centred system. 'I can't speak in any general way here because in Oxford, and at Cambridge to a lesser extent, women had a tremendous kick-start because the women's colleges employed only women and therefore there were bound to be women philosophers employed by the colleges. So in one way, one could get a good academic job without necessarily being very good at the subject, because this was a closed shop. This was one of the reasons why eventually the women's colleges began to employ male fellows before they took male undergraduates. So in Oxford, far from being at a disadvantage, in one way one could be said to be at an advantage.

'When the women's colleges went mixed – and this was the objection to going mixed that a lot of us had – we knew that that protected area would be eroded. Of course you could say that equally huge other fields would be opened up by the men's colleges. It's happened up to a point but not as much as one would like. There's by no means equality.'

Warnock also denies that many of the institutions and practices of academia, such as the adversarial seminar, are particularly suited to men.

'I've never known such adversarial people as women philosophers. I certainly don't think that they're little timid creatures that can't speak up in a seminar. Far from it – they sometimes dominate the scene. In fact, I would say the opposite. Women are rather garrulous. I see no symptoms of a male set-up.

'Take again my own case. I don't think I've ever suffered the faintest discrimination, but if what I've done is of rather modest value then that I think is an absolutely just judgement. I don't think anybody has ever judged me unduly harshly for my work. I haven't done very much work and I haven't done it very well. I think of myself as a very, very second-eleven, even third-eleven member of the profession. I think that a lot of women are in that position, for one reason or another, not unfairly, but that's where they belong.'

Even where Warnock admits that women are at a disadvantage,

she refuses to accept that it is due to any institutional sexism. For example, she says that 'increasingly academic jobs are awarded on the strength of the publications of the candidates, because the field is so strong. And it is a sad fact that young women publish less than young men because they're busy having children. They may catch up later, but just at the time when they are searching for jobs their publications list is usually less impressive.' What she does not do is draw the conclusion from this that jobs should be awarded on different criteria, or that academia should be more parent-friendly. For Warnock, the different demands on men and women just mean they will get on differently in their careers.

'I think that there's no doubt that women because of their usually divided lives – trying to keep everything going at the same time – tend to excel at subjects that take less time and probably less concentration. I know I'm talking autobiographically now. You can get away with much more if you take what I think of as the "soft subjects" in philosophy and therefore don't have to take hours in the library or even hours sitting when you are not to be disturbed as you work out a logical or mathematical problem.'

Warnock is most withering, however, about the claims of feminist philosophers that philosophical positions and arguments are essentially gendered. 'I find that, like all post-modernist positions, of which this one is a specimen, their propositions are so difficult to prove or disprove. In a way, it could be said to be self-refuting, contradictory, because they are putting forward this view, presumably, as a truth that is true for everybody and yet at the same time denying that there is any truth that is true for everybody. But at the same time they would claim that the point of view that they are expressing is just a particular point of view, namely a feminine one, and I find that a sort of frankly uninteresting proposition.

'I stick to that, though the heavens fall. It's not just philosophy I'm talking about. I believe that is true for all intellectual subjects. It may be the truth that you could find differences between women's approach and men's approach, but the aim of intellectual activity is to find the truth and I'm not going to take one single step down the post-modernist path which says there is no such thing as one truth. I feel very strongly about that.'

Does that mean that any differences there are that may come out empirically between the way women and men approach the subjects are obstacles but not absolute impediments on the road to truth?

'Absolutely. What they're aiming for is the same. That's the important point. For both men and women, the point is that they're trying to get things right. Somebody else from outside, a sociologist or a feminist, might find a different approach, but deliberately to set out to produce something which is women's only, that seems to me simply intellectually outrageous.'

The question of men and women taking different approaches to philosophy arises in Warnock's introduction to her anthology, where she noted how many postwar women philosophers have specialized in so-called applied philosophy, in particular ethics.

'I think it is the case that with the notable exception of Elizabeth Anscombe, most of the work done by women immediately after the War was in the subject of moral philosophy, and in moral philosophy they were increasingly realistic in that they were prepared to consider the way in which moral values are actually expressed and what the subject is actually about. I particularly think of Phillipa Foot who wrote several articles about rudeness, which is not the kind of subject that most men philosophers were prepared to interest themselves in.'

This was a radical change from a very detached form of ethics, which seemed to do its best not to say anything that might concern the real world, for instance to philosophers considering real-life ethical issues such as abortion and euthanasia. Why have women in particular been associated with that, at the time, revolutionary approach to moral philosophy?

'Well I think they've got more common sense on the whole than men and found it rather boring to go on and on and on about theoretical cases that did get rather ludicrous. Certainly in Oxford there was a school of philosophy which in a sense was realist because it thought you could just look at the world and see what things were right and wrong, but the sort of examples that those people took were all of the most trivial kind. I'm particularly thinking of Pritchard, who was a very influential philosopher in Oxford just before the War and whose books on moral philosophy were full of questions like whether you had a right to family news, whether you had fulfilled your duty by posting the letter or only if the letter had been received at the other end, and went on and on about setting yourself to post the letter. I think people like Phillipa Foot got fed up with it and thought, "Well, let's look at what really happens," and that was a very good move.'

But again, the most Warnock will concede is that 'women have been quite good at this kind of work'. Any suggestion that this is more than just a difference of temperament or aptitude is dismissed.

Given this radical resistance to any suggestion that there is anything interesting to say about women philosophers in particular, why did Warnock edit an anthology of women philosophers in the first place?

'I was asked to do it and said yes because I was in need of the money, which is my usual motive for writing or editing books. But I did warn the publishers that I was unlikely to come up with any tremendous solution and, of course, I was much blamed for not including all the feminist philosophy, which seemed to me intensely boring. So my motives were not very high. But I didn't realize until I'd actually done the work quite how difficult it was to come up with any genuine gender-related threads in philosophy. This rather pitiful thing about moral philosophy where one has to say that men did it just as well really, that was about it. I couldn't find anything else.'

It is not that Warnock didn't find the women philosophers interesting. Ann Conway, for example, really made an impression.

'I think Ann Conway was so mad that she didn't care what people thought. She had these amazing ideas which turned out to be very

like Leibniz's and may indeed have influenced Leibniz, but they seem to have come entirely out of her own head. She was a real original.'

However, on the whole, Warnock did not find too many of her women *philosophically* very interesting. Take Mary Wollstonecraft, for instance, the great campaigner and polemicist for women's rights.

'She really broke new ground, but in such a floundering way. She had no general theory of truth, she just told things as she saw them, which meant taking up the cause of, mainly, education. I thought quite a lot in Wollstonecraft – and again I think this is purely a historical point – was intended to apply equally to men and to women. The kind of society which she envisaged was one where everybody was educated equally, but the new form of education would be a kind of revolution just as much for men as for women. So though obviously women's education was defective in one way, men's education was equally defective in another, and she thought that the society that she envisaged of social and educational equality would be revolutionary for both sexes.'

If philosophers have a duty to speak the truth as they find it, and Warnock finds no truth in many of feminist philosophy's claims, does she deserve the criticism which so many male philosophers are spared? In being our most well-known woman philosopher, Mary Warnock's feminist credentials are held to account more than is perhaps fair. As she said, the only reason she holds the beliefs she does is that 'I couldn't find anything else'.

So perhaps it would be fairer to end with what Warnock has achieved rather than with the views she repudiates. Mary Warnock is one of only three philosophers in the House of Lords. Two out of the three are women, the other being Onora O'Neill. It says something for the achievement of Warnock's generation of women that, though they may not have the upper hand in academia, in public life they have had more visible success.

'Onora O'Neill and I are very much out of the same stable, though she's better in her work in philosophy than I am,' says Warnock. 'We've both very deliberately turned to public service and so we're there as a kind of statutory philosopher on a whole number of committees and commissions looking at moral issues. There's a huge rise in medical ethics and both of us in turn have sort of come to the fore as "practical philosophers". I think I regard Onora as my successor, and in our careers we ended up curiously parallel, one mistress of Girton and the other principal of Newnham. So I think if anyone thinks about us fifty years on we'll be thought to be identical twins.'

And two striking examples of how success comes differently to some women philosophers as compared to their male peers.

Selected Bibliography

Ethics Since 1900, 3rd edn (Oxford: Oxford University Press, 1978)
Imagination and Time (Oxford: Blackwell, 1994)
Women Philosophers, ed. (London: Everyman, 1996)
An Intelligent Person's Guide to Ethics (London: Duckworth, 1998)
A Memoir: People and Places (London: Duckworth, 2000)

16 The Dark Side

Ray Monk

Ray Monk has had an unusual career for a philosopher. A first-class degree from the University of York followed by an Oxford M.Litt thesis on Ludwig Wittgenstein's philosophy of mathematics would normally serve as the precursors to a doctorate and a lectureship. Monk, however, did not find the prospect of life as an academic philosopher very rewarding, and instead he opted to write an acclaimed biography of Wittgenstein.

Reviewers were almost universal in their praise for the book, which won the *Mail on Sunday*/John Llewellyn Rhys Prize in 1990. Monk then turned to Bertrand Russell, publishing two volumes of biography in 1996 and 2000. He also finally entered into academia and is now a professor of philosophy at the University of Southampton. With a professorship and three volumes of biography of twentieth-century British philosophy's most important figures under his belt, Monk has emerged as the only leading figure in British philosophy not to have got there by the standard route.

Yet his success has not been without its costs. His accounts of the lives of Wittgenstein and Russell show the good and the bad of both men, without being lurid. But the reviews got worse with each book: excellent for Wittgenstein, mixed for the first Russell volume, and often pretty vitriolic for the second. No little mud was slung Monk's way. Having revealed the dark side of two of philosophy's canonical figures, he himself saw the dark side of many of his contemporaries.

Monk has had some time to think about what lies behind this

'extremely strong' reaction. He's been helped by some comments Colin McGinn made at a conference on biography, before the second Russell volume had been published. Monk recalls: 'He said that when I described Wittgenstein doing things we don't particularly admire – like hitting a young girl until her nose bleeds, because she doesn't understand logic – people aren't going to get very upset about that, because it's extreme behaviour of the kind that people who are going to be asked to review these books would never do. They're fairly sober, mild-mannered, academic people who would never dream of hitting a girl because she doesn't understand logic. So they read this and it doesn't bother them. But when they read some of the things which Russell did, it's a bit closer to home. You see a description of Russell getting out of bed with one woman in order to write love letters to another woman, and you think, "hold on, this is the kind of thing I might do". So McGinn's explanation is that Russell's faults are closer to the faults of the people reviewing the books than Wittgenstein's faults are. I think there's something in that.'

On this diagnosis, Russell's failings were just too close for comfort. 'People weren't surprised to discover that Wittgenstein was driven by all kinds of things that they're not,' says Monk. 'Wittgenstein was a crazy Austrian foreigner. But Bertie Russell is one of us, and we can't entertain the notion that he was as driven and as close to the edge of insanity as Wittgenstein was. The picture of Wittgenstein as an intense man who's not quite like the rest of us, bordering on the insane, sat easily with people's perceptions, whether they admired him or not. But to represent Russell as driven in that way was to counter people's presuppositions.'

Monk also believes there's a political element to some of the criticism. 'If I say that this piece of political work is badly written, that it's a shoddy piece of work, and it happens to advocate a position, and someone reads it who advocates the same position, they're not going to separate the position from its shoddy presentation. If they approve of, let's say, nuclear disarmament, they're going to approve of a very eminent person advocating nuclear disarmament. They're not going to be too worried about whether the work supporting their cause is well written and well argued or not. So if I then come along and put the case for saying, whether one agrees with this position or not, this is just not a very good piece of work, the assumption will be that I'm opposed to that position. This came up in Michael Foot's response to the first volume. He wrote an introduction to Russell's autobiography which contained a sustained attack on my first volume. The assumption he seemed to be working with was that I was some kind of right-wing religious fanatic, because I evidently didn't admire, as he does, Russell as a left-wing secular saint.'

A third explanation for the vitriol hinges on people's expectations. 'What I was interested in was that in the case of Wittgenstein, the reviews were almost universally admiring, from people who both loved and hated him. The people who hated Wittgenstein said Monk has done a marvellous job of showing what a monster Wittgenstein was, and people who admired him said Monk has done a wonderful job of showing what a saint Wittgenstein was. In the case of Russell, it's the mirror image of that. People who hate him, Anthony Howard, for example, in the *Observer*, accused me of being sycophantic, of accepting without question Russell's perception of himself and so on. People who loved him have accused me of setting out from day one to assassinate his character. So there's a curious reversal going on there and I think it's to do with the fact that whether you love or hate Wittgenstein, the Wittgenstein I presented was the Wittgenstein you thought you loved or hated. In the case of Russell, the Russell I present is neither the one you hate nor the one you love.'

Monk is particularly irritated at the suggestion that he set out to do a hatchet job on Russell. 'Anthony Grayling accused me of that in his view in the *Guardian*. That's just wrong. Actually, Grayling's review was particularly nasty. He said that I got a large advance for it and that I knew even as I was banking the cheque that I loathed Russell. It's just not true. Some of the things that appalled me, most of them in fact, were discovered during the research.'

Despite the irritations of unfair reviews, Monk tries to keep it all in perspective. 'One can't take reviews very seriously,' he maintains, 'particularly the ones for the newspapers, because they're given so little time to do it. Someone will be sent this great big fat book and told, I want 800 words in three weeks' time. They've barely got time to read the book, let alone to think through a response to it.

'The other thing about reviews which is evident from the reviews of my book is the snowballing effect. With the Wittgenstein book, it just became the thing to do to praise the book. Now with the second volume of Russell, it's become the thing to do to point out that I hate Russell and that it's a biased, unbalanced book and so on. There's a kind of critical mass. Once it's been said a certain number of times, a reviewer feels more or less compelled to acknowledge this as a truth.'

One point made by some reviewers which Monk does seriously entertain is the possibility that there is a kind of exasperation that comes through in the second volume. The reader can get the feeling that Monk does lose a bit of patience with Russell by the end.

'I hope not but that's probably fair comment,' he concedes. 'Some of the people defending Russell haven't read this stuff. They've just said he's a very eminent man, he's made a stand for causes I believe in and therefore his stuff can't be as bad as Monk says. But if you read through 2,000 articles and you see him publishing on Tuesday something he contradicts on the Thursday, then exasperation does creep in. Alan Ryan took to me task in *The Times Literary Supplement*, but he wrote a political life of Bertrand Russell. He says the same thing there, that he hadn't read all of Russell's journalistic articles and that it was a dispiriting business reading as much of them as he did read, because they're just not very good.'

Does Monk think that his biographies undermine the idea that philosophers have a general ability to look the truth in the eye, and have a certain objectivity about things? This capacity certainly seems lacking in Russell, according to Monk's account of his life. He is portrayed as capable of both deception and self-deception.

Monk is not convinced that this is a particular weakness of philosophers. 'I think that's it's true of us generally that it's just hard work to take a long, honest, clear look at yourself.'

But isn't it the case that, although philosophers don't have a special problem in this regard, you might expect philosophers to be better than average at dealing with it? The fact that they're no worse than anyone else isn't much comfort. You'd expect that their whole training and *modus operandi* would make them more able to have that kind of objectivity, and they don't necessarily seem to.

'You wouldn't expect it exactly, because you know it's not true,' he responds. 'But one might feel that philosophers ought to be better at it. And I think this is what Wittgenstein thought in those remarks to Russell like, "how can I be a logician before I'm a decent human being?" If he's going to think clearly about logic, he's got to remove the things getting in the way of clear thought. Wittgenstein also said that in philosophy what is required is not intelligence but will. What's required to be honest about oneself is will. What did Russell lack when he fell into various forms of self-deception? It wasn't intelligence, it was strength of character.'

The idea that philosophy makes your life better has gained support recently with the growth of philosophical counselling and the success of Alain de Botton's *The Consolations of Philosophy* and its accompanying television series, *Philosophy: A Guide to Happiness*. Monk is not convinced by the claim that philosophy can make you happier in life.

'It's just obviously not true,' he says, incredulously. 'Philosophy doesn't make you happy and it shouldn't. Why should philosophy be consoling?'

I suggest that what de Botton and the philosophical counsellors might be doing is picking up on certain bits of philosophers and using them to derive comfort. So they're not really doing philosophy, they're simply making use of certain things in philosophy which might be consoling if you think about them in a certain way.

'That might have a purpose,' he replies, adding, 'if it does, great, but as you say, that's not philosophy.' But even here his scepticism is evident. He relates a recent experience when he was asked to take part in a radio discussion with the philosophical counsellor Lou Marinoff. Marinoff talked about a phone-in programme he was once on. 'He was asked by a mother of some teenage boys,' recalls Monk, 'how she could make her boys see that housework needs to be done and that it's unreasonable to expect her to do it all. How could she get her boys to tidy their rooms? Applying philosophy to this case, Marinoff said, you should remind your sons of Nietzsche's dictum that what doesn't kill me makes me stronger.'

Monk stops speaking there. He clearly thinks there's nothing more that needs to be said. The question of the value of a particular philosopher's work is not empty, however. Even if it doesn't make you happier, philosophy should be able to make you understand things better. Where does that leave philosophers like Wittgenstein, whose work is gnomic to say the least? Wittgenstein himself doesn't seem to doubt that his work is important but also difficult to understand. He says things such as that there are only one or two people who really understand what he's saying. This presents at least two problems: the first one is, how do we know his inscrutability is not a sign that his philosophy is just confused, rather than profound? Second, if his work is so hard to understand, why is there such a Wittgenstein industry, with all these people claiming to have understood him? If you take seriously Wittgenstein's own claim that very few people understand him, how does that affect Monk's own confidence in his ability to understand him himself?

'I don't suppose for a moment that if Wittgenstein were alive today he would number me among the two or three people who understood his work. Nevertheless, I have a deep interest in his work, and I can share that interest with other people, so I don't think what I'm doing is completely without value. Do I completely understand Wittgenstein? Probably not. Would I be identified by him as somebody who understood him? Certainly not.'

But given this lack of understanding, how does one know whether Wittgenstein's philosophy is difficult but profound, or obscurantist and shallow?

'On the basis of whether it works for you,' replies Monk. 'Does this make what you're thinking about clearer? It seemed to me that in a lot of cases with the later Wittgenstein's work the answer is yes. In more or less technical issues such as logical form, but also on more general issues, it seems to me that the anti-scientism which is a passion of Wittgenstein's later work and throughout his life is an increasingly valuable message in our culture.'

One issue raised by philosophical biography is the extent to which the personality of a thinker can be separated from beliefs or arguments. In one sense at least, acknowledging the role of personality does not threaten the idea of truth.

'It might be true that only a certain type of personality would bother spending ten years working on *Principia Mathematica*, with the passion that Russell did,' explains Monk. 'You might say, "look, Bertie, get a life", that this is replacing something, this is a substitute for something. And yet it could still be the case that what he says is true. It is a pursuit of truth but it's a pursuit of truth of a kind that only a particular kind of personality would bother with.'

But there is a deeper worry. Good reasoning can lead you to some surprising conclusions. Faced with this, we can make one of two choices. We can say that this is a valid and sound argument so we must accept the surprising conclusion, or we can say that something must have gone wrong with our reasoning, that though we appear to have reasoned well, we must have reasoned badly because we end up with an absurd conclusion. Here, we say the argument is not sound but a *reductio ad absurdum*. In any individual case, how do we know if we have a sound argument with a surprising conclusion or a reduction?

'Whether it's a sound argument or a *reductio* will depend on how obviously unacceptable the conclusion is,' is Monk's first reply. But isn't the worry raised by philosophical biography that how obviously unacceptable the conclusion is will depend partly on things like temperament, which might seem to threaten philosophy's self-image as an objective discipline?

'Perhaps,' says Monk. 'Russell's career throws up examples of this. Russell did indeed develop an argument that he thought was sound, to the effect that the only things we can see, the only things we can know, the only things we can have direct acquaintance with, are the things literally inside our heads. Most people would think that once you've got there, something has gone very wrong with your reasoning.

'There's another example in the philosophy of language in the 1930s. Russell developed a causal theory of meaning and he was challenged by Braithwaite, who asked why, if the causal theory is true, am I not caused to utter the word "cow" whenever I see a cow? Russell's reply to this was that, I don't know about you, but whenever I see a cow, I feel an involuntary movement in my larynx. It is a feature of Russell's style that he is willing to accept absurdities because the argument seems to be leading there, and he thinks that's a virtue – the rejection of common sense. As he once put it, common sense is the metaphysics of savages. Is that a temperamental thing? Yes, but it would be a difficult job to explain the ways in which it was a temperamental thing. But certainly people vary with regard to what they're prepared to swallow on the basis of an argument.

'Also I think this throws up an interesting difference in the way people argue. Wittgenstein once commented on some lectures which Broad gave at Cambridge where he ran through styles of philosophy. He characterized the Kantian style as saying, "we know certain things about the world, that's not in doubt, now let's look at what's required in order for us to know those things". Wittgenstein commented on that and said yes, that's the right method. Russell would have said that's exactly the wrong method. You start from things which cannot be false, you proceed validly and you end with things that cannot be false.'

But in deciding which of these methods we are to adopt, it seems that we're not left with anything other than which way we feel suits us better. There's no way of adjudicating between them.

'I don't know if there's no way of adjudicating, but certainly it can't be on the basis of a valid argument, because what we're discussing here is the basis of validity itself. Whether we have to immediately retreat and say it's just a temperamental thing, I'm not sure. It may be that there is some kind of reasoning that would persuade you to adopt a Wittgensteinian or Kantian method rather than a Russellian method, which stopped short of being a valid argument. Clearly when one's discussing what criteria of validity to adopt, claiming a valid argument is going to be begging the question.

'But that wouldn't put a stop to all forms of reasoning. One thing that is important to bear in mind in the sort of things we've been talking about is what a limited weapon a valid argument is and how rare it is that we're persuaded to believe something or adopt something on the basis of a valid argument.'

However much reading Monk's biographies lessens one's trust in the judgement of great thinkers, it certainly does not devalue their work.

'The advantage with philosophy is that one doesn't have to take it on trust. Just read the work. The value of *Principles of Mathematics* as a contribution to philosophy is not at all undermined by the fact that in his old age Russell wrote a load of nonsense about the impact the United States was having on international affairs. The fact that he's very weak on international affairs doesn't undermine what he has to say about the relation between logic and mathematics. It's not as though those things are completely separate, it's just that the one doesn't provide a basis for judging the other. One could say, I think, that the weakness of character which is revealed in his willingness to publish a lot of rubbish about politics is not entirely separate from the sides of his personality that enabled him to work with such impressive concentration on logic and mathematics.'

It is tracing these interplays between life and thought which makes the biographies of Ray Monk so interesting to read, and evidently to write as well. Those who think that only the ideas of philosophers count and that their lives are irrelevant should think again.

Selected Bibliography

Ludwig Wittgenstein: The Duty of Genius (London: Jonathan Cape, 1990)
Bertrand Russell, Volume 1: The Spirit of Solitude (London: Jonathan Cape, 1996)
Bertrand Russell, Volume 2: The Ghost of Madness (London: Jonathan Cape, 2000)

V   Metaphysics

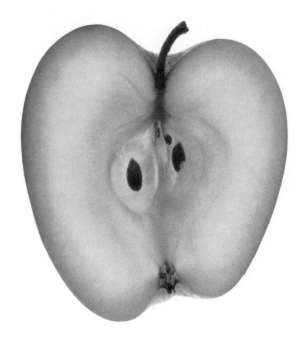

17 Free Will

Ted Honderich

In 35 years at University College London, Grote Professor Emeritus Ted Honderich has written important work on a wide range of philosophical topics. These include punishment's supposed justifications, causation, John Stuart Mill, terrorism, equality, Anomalous Monism, conservatism, consequentialism, the subjectivity of the mind, consciousness as existence, the mind–brain relation, and the nature of actions. He has also written a strikingly honest and critically acclaimed autobiography, *Philosopher: A Kind of Life*. However, it is perhaps for his work on determinism, and for thinking that determinism is true, that he is best known. So I begin by asking him what he takes determinism to be.

'Determinism, as I understand it,' he answers, 'is the doctrine that each of our mental or conscious events or episodes, including every decision, choice and action, is the effect of a certain kind of causal sequence. The sequence goes back a long way in time before the decision, choice or action and any thought about it. Also, the sequence is one of standard causation. Each event in it is a real effect – a necessary event, so to speak. Certainly not an event merely made probable by antecedents. It is something that had to happen given the antecedents as they were. Determinism, so defined, isn't itself the doctrine that we are not free – that question is not touched on in this definition.'

For a person not familiar with the free will and determinism debate, it will perhaps not be immediately clear why determinism does not entail the assertion that we are not free. So I ask Honderich what the thought is here.

'Well, it's been felt to be an open question whether or not freedom is inconsistent with such a doctrine of determinism,' he replies. 'There are philosophers – at one time they seemed to be a majority in philosophy in the English language – who have taken the view that determinism and freedom are logically consistent, that determinism can be true and yet we can still be perfectly and entirely free. So it's a good idea – anyway convenient – to leave anything about freedom out of a definition of determinism itself.'

The philosophical position that determinism and freedom are logically consistent is normally called 'Compatibilism'. This position depends upon distinguishing between what Honderich calls voluntary and originated actions. What, I ask, is involved in this distinction?

'The kind of freedom that is voluntariness amounts to this: a free action is one that flows from the desires, personality and character of the agent, rather than being somehow against those things. The agent is not in jail, not the victim of a man with a gun, not subject to an inner compulsion he wants not to have. He is acting in such a way that his actions in a clear sense flow from himself. A free action by this definition is indeed logically consistent with determinism. Determinism doesn't say that there are no actions that flow from the agent. It just says that there is *some* causal background that fixes the outcome. A free action on the Compatibilist account is just one that has a certain kind of causal background – internal and fundamental to the agent, so to speak, rather than external.

'As for origination,' Honderich continues, 'it comes from the opposing tradition in philosophy that maintains that a free action is inadequately defined by the Compatibilists. For the Incompatibilists, a free action is a voluntary one but also much more than that. It is one that has a certain genesis, a certain inception, rather difficult to define. In one sense, we know what Incompatibilists take origination to be. It's the agent coming to a decision, choice or action in such a way that determinism is not true of this, and yet the decision, choice or action remaining within the control of the agent. Above all, origination is a beginning of a decision or choice that makes the agent responsible for it – morally responsible for it in a certain strong sense. Free actions, if they are not only voluntary but also originated, are certainly inconsistent with determinism. If determinism is true, there aren't any of these free actions.'

The notion of origination then seems to be that free actions are not determined, they remain within the control of the agent and the agent is morally responsible for them. However, it is extremely difficult to imagine what these actions might be like, so is the concept coherent?

'Many philosophers have said there is the greatest difficulty about arriving at a clear conception of origination,' he admits. 'Part of the difficulty is that an originated decision, if there are any, is one that could have been different at the very moment it is made. If I decide this morning to write something insulting about Tony Blair, I can at that moment decide to act differently. What this means is that the past could have been exactly as it was up until that moment and I can nonetheless decide differently. That story contains within it a pretty alarming proposition, or so it seems – namely that *there is no standard explanation of the decision I in fact make.* You would have to look for such a thing in the present and past circumstances. But in both of these places, as you've just heard, everything could have been the same and I could have decided differently. So in one clear sense it appears there is no possibility of any explanation whatever of this decision that was made.'

However, Honderich does not believe that origination is a null notion.

'After all,' he says, 'I can define it right now as the giving-rise to a decision in such a way that the decision is not determined, and yet is within the control of the agent, and moreover such that he is really responsible for it. I haven't said *nothing* when I've said that. I haven't said something incoherent. Admittedly I haven't explained how there can be such decisions, but I have said something that appears to make sense. Indeed, what we have here is an idea or conception in common usage. People regularly think after someone has behaved very badly, maybe viciously, that the person could at the final moment have not done the thing, given things just as they were. So the idea of origination, even if it does contain a mystery, does exist. Sense can be given to it, and it seems to be entrenched in ordinary culture – anyway Western culture as we know it.'

Of course, it is one thing to accept that this notion is coherent, it is quite another to maintain that it is true or plausible. One particular problem is that it is difficult to see how agents can escape the network of causality which seems to exist with respect to all other phenomena in the natural world.

'I agree with you that there is no origination,' Honderich responds, 'but that doesn't commit me to thinking there doesn't exist any conception of origination. There can certainly be false conceptions – including important ones – and there certainly *can* be conceptions that are partly mysterious. There are lots of them. What you and I think is true is determinism, but we are in a minority. Most people are inclined to think that determinism is false. They talk of Free Will and have in mind something like the origination we've been talking about – anyway a kind of image along those lines. Also, there are a lot of more informed characters about who have heard of Quantum Theory, the physics of the twentieth century. They think it refutes determinism.'

The Quantum Theory defence of free will is popular. It rests on the claim that the indeterminacy which seems to exist at the level of quantum events somehow lets in the possibility of non-determined choices. But Honderich is not convinced.

'My own resistance to this idea that Quantum Theory falsifies determinism has got a number of parts, of which the following are two.

'Firstly, if there really is indeterminism – uncaused events, events that aren't effects – then they are of course at a micro-level, well below the level, for example, of brain events that go with choices and decisions. More important, they don't translate upwards to the macro-level. That is our experience. We don't see miraculous little events, chance events, like spoons levitating. We ought to have this evidence if the miraculous micro-events come up to the top. So a first resistance to the Quantum Theory stuff is that if determinism is true, it's irrelevant.

'A second resistance is to there actually being any of the events in question, down at the micro-level. All the popular books about Quantum Theory, some of them by distinguished physicists, say one thing. It is that you can't carry over old assumptions from classical physics into contemporary and recent physics. One of the things that you can't carry over is a conception of the nature of the things that before Quantum Theory used to be said to be caused or determined. For example, it is said that if the term "particle" is used in an interpretation of Quantum Theory, you are not to suppose a particle is a small bit of matter in the Newtonian way. It is very uncertain in the end, and indeed this is admitted by most exponents of Quantum Theory, *what* the things are that are said not to be effects. Sometimes they are taken to be probabilities or possibilities or indeed propositions.

'The essential point here is that it looks like the things that we are told are not effects, are things that the determinist never said were effects. No sensible determinist has said that numbers – say the numbers 4 and 5 – are effects, or that propositions are effects. These are thought to be abstract objects and no one has supposed that the determinist is committed to saying that these are effects. Or that one end of an equation is an effect of the other end. Determinism, plainly, is only about *events*, or a certain class of *events*. In short, to repeat, it's very possible that the things that are asserted in Quantum Theory not to be effects are in fact not events at all, and are therefore not relevant to determinism.'

The importance of Ted Honderich's 1988 book, *A Theory of Determinism: The Mind, Neuroscience, and Life-Hopes*, and the first edition of his introductory summary of it, *How Free Are You?*, translated into seven languages, was not only that it made the case for determinism. It also moved the debate forward beyond between Compatibilism and Incompatibilism.

'I actually believe I've proved both are false,' says Honderich. 'Is any philosopher allowed one moment of pomposity? I'll use mine up here.'

He explains why. 'What my stuff comes to can be put in terms of life-hopes, certain attitudes to the future. We all have them. These are large hopes about the working out of our lives. They have to do with our future actions and what will flow from those actions. What is most important, however, is that these particular attitudes come in two kinds. You can discover the two kinds in yourself.

'I can feel about the future in a way that makes it bright. The essential point is that I can have an attitude to it as something in which I will get what I want, where I'll be doing what I want. I'll end up with the right person, or with money, or just healthy, or whatever. I won't be alone or in jail or bed-ridden and so on. Things will turn out in accord with my desires, needs, personality and nature. If I'm in this way of feeling, furthermore, I can feel that determinism can turn out to be true, and it won't matter much. All of us have this kind of hope, or at the very least can get into it.

'On the other hand, almost all of us have or can get into a very different sort of hope. It's to the effect that we're going to be able to rise up over our pasts, rise over our characters, rise over our weaknesses, and defeat the things which have kept us back – anyway to some extent. Our futures aren't written down waiting to be read, fixed already. This is a hope, further, that is wrecked if we think of determinism as true.

'That we have or can have both these attitudes shows that we have both the conception of free actions as just voluntary, and the conception of free actions as both voluntary and originated. The first conception, plainly, is in the first sort of hope, and the second conception is in the second sort. Both these ideas are within us. If that is true, then both Compatibilism and Incompatibilism are false. They are both false because they agree in one thing – that each of us has one single settled conception of a free action. Look at Hume in the eighteenth century. Look at van Inwagen in the twentieth. The Compatibilists say that our idea is voluntariness and the Incompatibilists that it is voluntariness plus origination. They're both up the spout.

'There is also another kind of plain proof of our having the two ideas,' continues Honderich. 'There's a public behavioural proof. Think of declarations and codes of rights – a body of human rights or just legal rights of some kind. What they try to secure is that people will be voluntary in their lives – not compelled or coerced by other people. These codes aim at liberties that have nothing to do with origination. But other practices we have, some of them in the law, plainly do have to do with origination or free will. And we give ourselves a standing higher than the animal kingdom or the rest of the animal kingdom partly by this means.'

But is there no problem at all about determinism and freedom? Honderich agreed in the two books that there was, and also took himself to have dealt with it.

'If Compatibilism and Incompatibilism are both false, the real problem of determinism of course isn't what our single shared idea of freedom is – we've got two. The real problem of determinism is living with and somehow emerging from the situation where we've got two conceptions of freedom and they enter into important attitudes and practices that we have – our life-hopes and a good deal more.'

If Honderich is right about our having two conceptions of freedom and also the various attitudes that go with them, I wonder why it is that we don't seem to have certain kinds of attitudes – for example, retributive attitudes – towards non-biological machines. After all, it is at least arguable that non-biological machines satisfy the criteria for voluntariness. And also determinism seems to turn *us* into biological machines, if it is true. So why when a machine acts to benefit us greatly do we not feel a certain kind of gratitude, for example?

'I agree that we don't have certain attitudes in connection with machines. When they benefit us, we don't have certain desires to do well by them in return, if only by saying thanks. We don't have the counterparts of the retributive desires we may have if a person wounds us. I take it the short explanation, or the first part of the explanation, is that these machines aren't conscious. Doesn't something have to be conscious to be voluntary or to originate something?'

For Honderich, the real problem of trying to live with determinism involved three possible responses: *dismay*, *intransigence* and *affirmation*. I ask him what these involve.

'Dismay is a response to determinism that may have to do with life-hopes, claims or feelings of knowledge, personal feelings, moral approval and disapproval and so on. Dismay is the response that if determinism is true, these things are wrecked. My life-hopes must collapse, and so on. I can't be confident in what I used to call my knowledge. I can't engage in gratitude or resentment. I can't hold people responsible.

'Intransigence is the response that if determinism is true I can still soldier on – with my life-hopes, personal feelings and so on.

'The first of these responses comes from concentrating on the conception of freedom as not only voluntariness but also origination, which is inconsistent with determinism. Intransigence comes from the conception of freedom as just voluntariness.

'Being inclined to both these responses is no happy thing. You're in a kind of conflict situation for a start.

'What is needed is to make the response of *affirmation*, which you might think boils down to getting rid of desires that cannot be satisfied if determinism is true, and being as fulfilled as possible in the fact that other desires can still be satisfied. Something better can be said along those lines. Affirmation can be the response that life can be great and fulfilling. As for the giving up on the other desires, the best way to succeed in it is to come to believe in determinism.'

That was Honderich's resolution to the real problem of determinism in the first edition of *How Free Are You?* and its large predecessor. But in his recent autobiography, he owns up to finding it hard to give up the idea that he has more responsibility for his life than is allowed by determinism. He allows he has sharp feelings of responsibility and a sense of his life – at least like the feelings and the sense tied to a belief in origination.

'But the solution isn't to go back to indeterminism,' he insists. 'It can't be. Another thing that can happen when you think of your past life is that you can become *more* convinced of determinism. It seems to me that we need a really different view of our lives, a radically different one. We have to forget about tinkering with origination. There is some *individuality* about each of our lives that has a basis in something else, something totally different.

'It may have a basis in the nature of our consciousness, anyway our perceptual consciousness – being aware of the room you're in for a start. If something called Consciousness as Existence is true, each of us is a kind of constructor or part-constructor of reality. That's pretty individual, isn't it?

'And it could be there's a kind of explanation of what we do that is different from anything about origination and consistent with determinism and yet not the Compatibilist story. It has to do with a paradox about causal explanation. We rightly think the presence of oxygen is just as necessary to your writing the fatal resignation letter as your ideas about the insult – they're both required conditions. But somehow the ideas are more explanatory. It could be we can get something out of this in connection with the sense of our lives. We somehow run our own lives.'

Selected Bibliography

Punishment: The Supposed Justifications (Harmondsworth: Penguin, 1971)
Philosopher: A Kind of Life (London: Routledge, 2000)
How Free Are You?, 2nd edn (Oxford: Oxford University Press, 2002)
The Determinism and Freedom Philosophy website:
    http://www.homepages.ucl.ac.uk/~uctytho

18 Realism

John Searle

John Searle is without a doubt one of the most eminent philosophers of our time. He has been president of the American Philosophical Association, the BBC Reith Lecturer, a Guggenheim Fellow, and has twice won a Fulbright Award. Now Mills Professor of the Philosophy of Mind and Language at the University of California, Berkeley, he spent his formative years in the 1950s in Oxford. The influence of the Oxford philosopher of language J. L. Austin, inventor of the term 'speech acts', is evident in the title of Searle's first book, *Speech Acts: An Essay in the Philosophy of Language*. But although his philosophy may have its origins in the ordinary-language philosophy of Austin's Oxford, in its scope and ambition it grew into something much more. Language is just the start.

When Searle turned to the philosophy of mind, he came up with perhaps the most famous counterexample in history – the Chinese room argument – and in one intellectual punch inflicted so much damage on the then dominant theory of functionalism that many would argue it has never recovered. More recently, he has tried to establish what he calls a new branch of philosophy – the philosophy of society.

Recently, Searle has had a certain preoccupation with bringing together the various strands of his philosophy over the last thirty-odd years. It has always been possible to trace the continuities in his thought, but in his recent books like *Mind, Language and Society* and

Rationality in Action, Searle himself has been making the connections and presenting his work as a coherent system.

Mind, Language and Society: Philosophy in the Real World is his second attempt at writing for a wider audience. It follows the success, both critical and commercial, of his 1984 *Minds, Brains and Science*, which was based on his Reith lectures.

'I like to communicate my ideas,' says Searle. 'There are three reasons. One is it is a tremendous intellectual discipline. I discovered this when I was doing the Reith lectures. In general I feel if you can't say it clearly you don't understand it yourself. So partly it's for my own benefit. It forces me into the kind of discipline needed to make my ideas as clear as possible.

'The second thing is it enables us to reach a larger audience. I think the most exciting questions in the world are philosophical questions, and I think there's no reason why we shouldn't tell the general public the excitement we have from doing philosophy. If you can write a book that's totally clear, then you can get that across to the general public.

'The third point is that the intellectual weaknesses in your own ideas are much more obvious. You're able to make progress better if you can see the strength and limitations of your own view, but you can't do that if it's all stated obscurely.'

Searle admits, however, that if you write for a popular audience, 'you also pay a price, which annoys me. People will attack the Reith lectures, where they can twist things around to suit their interpretation, whereas if they looked at some longer work of mine, like *The Rediscovery of the Mind*, they'd find they were misunderstanding me. So you do pay a price for stating it simply, namely it's easier for the professionals to misunderstand.'

Mind, Language and Society brought together for the first time the various aspects of Searle's thought, and in doing so gave a clear picture of his realism – a belief in the real existence of a world independent of us. His general motivation for this is the conviction that 'you make a terrible mistake in philosophy if you go around denying things that are obviously true and go around saying things that are obviously false, and it seems to me obviously false to say that the real world only exists because we think about it or because we construct it. I actually think that denial is a kind of bad faith, it's a kind of will to power. It's the idea that somehow or other reality is responsible to us, rather than us being answerable to a real world. When I debated with Richard Rorty, Richard would not say that he denies the existence of the real world, but on this specific point he said, "Why should we be responsible to anything? It's up to us."'

Searle's realism is most strong when it comes to the existence of the external world.

'I am mostly concerned in my latest book to defend a view I call "external realism",' he explains, 'the idea that there is a real world that exists independently of our perceptions, our thoughts, feelings and attitudes. You might think that was so obvious that no sane person would deny it, but there's a whole army of people out there denying it.'

This can sound like a simple appeal to common sense, but Searle insists 'that's never my argument. I suppose common sense would say that the world is flat and we each have a mind and a body. Both of those are false. It's just that, as a matter of fact, we've been on this planet for quite a while, and there are some things we know. One of the things we know, for example, is that all of our mental processes are caused by processes in the brain. That's the kind of starting point I can take when I work in the philosophy of mind. Similarly, I want to start with the idea that if we engage in discourse, you and I, and we agree, for example, that we're going to meet in a certain place to have a conversation, we take it for granted that there's a reality that exists independently of us. I don't say that's a common-sense belief. On the contrary, I insist that that's really something prior to belief, that the presupposition of an independently existing reality is what I call a background presupposition. It's not something that's up for grabs in the way that whether or not the human genome project will have such and such an effect is.

'Then the question is, well what do you do with all the challenges to that view? And I attack those. I don't defend the idea that there's a reality so much as I criticize the attacks on it, and I point out that it plays a certain role in our background presupposition, because it's what we take for granted when we engage in discourse.'

But is to say that the real existence of the external world is a presupposition or background theory just a convenient way of getting him off the hook of having to argue for it?

'Not quite,' he replies, 'because it makes it almost impossible to argue for it. I do offer a transcendental argument for it. I show that you can't engage in normal discourse without that presupposition. So if you think that normal discourse is meaningful in the way we suppose it to be, then you're already committed to the presupposition. That's a kind of transcendental argument: assume that our normal discourse functions the way we take it to function, then it follows that external realism must be right.

'To nail this down to examples. You and I made an arrangement to meet at a certain place at a certain time. We couldn't make that and we couldn't have our normal understanding of that unless we assume there is a place in space and in time that is independent of us and we can meet at that particular place. That is external realism.'

So how does Searle deal with the attacks on external realism? One such challenge is perspectivism, the view that we can only talk about reality from one perspective. Searle seems to regard that as not a devastating challenge to realism but merely as a trite truism.

'Yeah,' agrees Searle, 'I think these guys make an obvious fallacy where they infer from the fact that all knowledge is from a point of view, from a certain perspective, that therefore the only thing that exists is perspectives. That doesn't follow. I mean, you see this table from your point of view, I see it from my point of view, but there's a table that exists from no point of view.'

But isn't the crux of the argument that the table from no point of view is unknowable?

'Well I think that's right. Traditionally, the argument that most people have found for the denial of realism, certainly in the philosophical tradition that you and I have been brought up in, is an epistemic argument. As Berkeley says, if matter exists we could never know it; if it doesn't exist everything remains the same. It's an epistemically unknowable entity. I want to say, no, it's not unknowable at all. That's just a certain misconception of the nature of perception – we assume that if matter exists we can never have any perceptual access to it. Of course we can.

'There's a deeper objection I have to this whole tradition and that is that I think our obsession with epistemology was a 300-year mistake. Descartes set us off on this and we just have to get out of the idea that the main aim of philosophy is to answer scepticism. There are all sorts of much more interesting questions. I don't take scepticism seriously. I take it seriously in the way I take Zeno's paradoxes seriously – they're nice puzzles. But when I hear about Zeno's paradoxes I don't think, "Oh my God, maybe space and time don't exist." I think, "That's an interesting paradox, let's work it out." That's how I feel about the sceptical paradoxes. I don't feel that they show that the real world doesn't exist or that we can never have knowledge of it. I'm quite stunned, in a way, that we've had three hundred years of taking scepticism that seriously.

'My friends who are serious epistemologists think that I'm just unmusical where scepticism is concerned. They think there's some deep truth there that I'm missing. I don't see it. I think these are interesting puzzles and paradoxes but now once we get through worrying about them we can get down and go to work on the serious constructive parts of philosophy. The really exciting parts of philosophy are the constructive parts where we want to construct a theory: a theory of the mind, a theory of language, in my case a theory of social reality.'

A further challenge is from the 'underdetermination of theories by evidence'. Searle minces no words in his analysis of this argument.

'It's the usual thing in philosophy where you go from something platitudinous to something preposterous. The platitudinous point is perfectly legitimate, namely, that given any amount of data, there are alternative and inconsistent theories that will be consistent with all the evidence. So there's no algorithm, given the evidence, that would tell you what is the correct theory. You just use the evidence as a way of testing your theory, but the evidence doesn't fix the theory, because you can have different theories that are consistent with all of the evidence.

'That's one point. But then a lot of people want to make the next move and they want to say, well there really isn't any fact of the matter. There's just the evidence. There isn't any real world that the evidence is about.'

Searle quotes as an 'egregious example of this' Quine's famous argument about indeterminacy. Quine argues that there is no fact of the matter about meanings, because there is always a gap between the evidence for what someone means when they make an utterance and what it could mean. Quine uses the example of someone talking about a rabbit. When I hear someone say 'look at that rabbit', the term 'rabbit' could refer to the rabbit as a being whose existence stretches from birth to death or it could refer to only that particular life-stage of the rabbit present when I make the utterance. Both interpretations of my term 'rabbit' are consistent with the evidence provided by my utterance.

Searle believes that Quine is 'confusing the underdetermination of theory by evidence with the idea that the theory isn't really about any matter of fact. Of course there's a matter of fact about what I mean, about whether or not I mean "rabbit" or "stage in the life history of the rabbit", and the conclusive case which Quine never considers is the first-person case. That is, I know exactly that I mean "rabbit" not "stage in the life history of a rabbit" when I say "rabbit". I couldn't even state Quine's theory of indeterminacy if I couldn't make that distinction.'

Given such strong realist leanings, the title of another of his books, *The Construction of Social Reality,* is surprising. How can a realist talk about any reality being constructed? Searle's account of social reality in this book, reprised in *Mind, Language and Society*, reveals a subtler realist than some of Searle's more bullish pronouncements might suggest.

'The key element in the construction of the kind of social reality that I am interested in,' explains Searle, 'is that human beings have the capacity to impose functions on things. The result is that those things cannot perform the function without collective acceptance or recognition of the things as having a certain status. An obvious example is money. It only works because we accept it – we accept these bits of paper and bits of metal as money. The way that they differ from, for example, a wall is that a wall can perform its function by virtue of its physical structure – it's just too high to climb over. But if you just make a line on the ground and say "this is the boundary", the boundary can only perform its function if it is accepted or recognized as a boundary. I say that's the key element in understanding institutional reality: there's a class of objectively existing facts in the world that are only the facts they are because we collectively recognize them as such, and that goes with prime ministers, governments, marriage, private property, universities, professorships, conferences and the English language. They're all very important in our life but they are all cases of "status-functions" – where the fact can only perform the function in virtue of collective acceptance or recognition.'

Searle's account of status-functions seems unproblematic, but what added purchase is given by saying they are objective? What if a person says, 'I accept everything you say about how we have money, but I want to say it's subjectively real, not objectively real'?

'I want to distinguish between two different senses of the objective/subjective distinction,' replies Searle. 'There is an ontological sense where, for example, mountains have an objective mode of existence and pains have a subjective mode of existence. That's ontological subjectivity and objectivity. But also there's an epistemic distinction between subjectivity and objectivity. For example, I think that Wittgenstein was a better philosopher than Russell. Well, there's a subjective element in that. I think that Wittgenstein died in England, that's epistemically objective. So in addition to the distinction between ontological subjectivity and objectivity you have an epistemic distinction, epistemic objectivity and subjectivity.

'Now here's the point: institutional facts do have an ontologically subjective component. They're only the facts they are because we think that they are. But that doesn't prevent them from being epistemically objective. It's just an objective fact, epistemically speaking, that this piece of paper in my hand is a five-pound note. That is, it isn't just my opinion that it's a five-pound note. If I go into a store and I try to buy something with this, they don't say, "well maybe you think it's money but who cares what you think", so it's epistemically objective. But of course, the fact that this paper functions as money has an element in it which is ontologically subjective. So I want to insist that epistemic objectivity is perfectly consistent with ontological subjectivity.'

Does that imply that there's a false idea of objectivity which we've got to get rid of, that is, to say that something is objectively the case means that it must continue to be so regardless of what we do?

'That's right,' confirms Searle, 'because there's an ontologically subjective component in the existence of all institutional reality: money, property, marriage, government and all the rest of it.'

Searle is evangelical about spreading the study of such areas. 'This is fascinating to me, partly because I think this is a neglected area in philosophy. Most philosophers have this dumb inventory of problems that they've inherited from reading whoever and I want to say there are all these problems out there that whoever didn't write about. If we want to give a coherent account of reality we've got to account for how social and institutional reality fits into our overall theories from physics.

'I think we need to invent a new branch of philosophy, which I want to call the philosophy of society. We already have something called social and political philosophy, but that tends to be about political philosophy really. I think that just as we have a philosophy of language and a philosophy of mind, we should have a philosophy of society, and social and political philosophy will fall out of that quite naturally, as will the methodology of the social sciences. But the basic subject matter of the philosophy of society is the ontology and logical structure of social reality, just as the basic subject matter of philosophy of language is the ontology and logical structure of speech acts and other linguistic phenomena. This subject doesn't exist. I'm trying to bring it to birth.'

Perhaps the most surprising feature of *Mind, Language and Reality* is a small comment he drops inconspicuously at the end of the book, that he wants to build an adequate *general* theory. Historically, general theories tend to be associated with the metaphysicians, the rationalists and particularly the idealists. Searle is more of an empiricist, a pragmatic, a realist. Those kinds of philosophers have tended to prefer an analytic, piecemeal approach, particularly in the twentieth century.

'When I was in Oxford,' says Searle, 'the term piecemeal was a term of praise. What we wanted were little bitty results. We were suspicious of large results. But I think that was due to the fact that philosophers who wanted large results had done such a bad job. I don't think it was in the nature of the subject matter and I don't agree that the empiricist philosophers had been opposed to general theories. I think Hume very much had a general theory, Locke had a general theory, even Berkeley in his way had a general theory. So I think that in intellectual life you should never be just satisfied with bits and pieces of information and understanding. You want to know how it all hangs together. That is one of the great achievements of Western civilization.

'My own view, and I'm certainly no scholar, is that that's the greatest invention of the Greeks – the idea of a theory. The actual theories that they come up with are probably in most respects pretty feeble, but the idea that you had a systematic set of propositions, logically related to each other which could account for a whole domain, that's a wonderful idea. Euclid's elements is one of the classics. Aristotle's full of theories. That's what I want. I want a theory in the classical, Greek, Aristotelian sense.'

So Searle is also reclaiming the general theory for the realist, welcoming it back to its natural home, for surely it is the realist who would most expect the various components of understanding to fit together.

'They'd better,' says Searle.

Selected Bibliography

Minds, Brains and Science (Cambridge, MA: Harvard University Press, 1984)
The Rediscovery of the Mind (Cambridge, MA: MIT Press, 1992)
The Construction of Social Reality (New York: The Free Press, 1995)
Mind, Language and Society: Philosophy in the Real World (New York: Basic Books, 1998)
Rationality in Action (Cambridge, MA: MIT Press, 2001)

19 Beyond Realism and Anti-realism

Jonathan Rée

There is a certain caricature of philosophers which has it that they spend their time arguing about whether things like tables and chairs exist. This *is* just a caricature, but nevertheless there is an element of truth in it when it comes to the debate about realism and anti-realism. Put crudely, realists – or, more precisely, *external realists* – think both that the world exists independently of our perceptions of it and thoughts about it, and that we can reliably know about the world. Anti-realists, for a variety of reasons, doubt both these propositions.

The philosophical debate about realism and anti-realism – which involves arguments about, for example, sense experience, language, and the nature of knowledge – is complex and esoteric. However, in recent times, as Jonathan Rée points out, it has found more public expression in the concern that scientists have about the way that their endeavours are treated by the humanities.

In fact, this is a long-standing concern. It was in 1959 that C. P. Snow gave his famous lecture on 'The Two Cultures', in which he expressed dismay at the division between the arts and the sciences, and the hostility with which the practitioners of each viewed the other. It appeared to him that 'the intellectual life of the whole of Western society... [was] increasingly being split into two polar groups'. This he considered both culturally and politically damaging.

More than forty years on, the divide and hostility remain. These came to the fore a few years ago in *l'affaire Sokal*. Inspired by what he saw as the obscurity and ambiguity of much post-modernist writing, the physicist Alan Sokal hoaxed the journal *Social Text* into publishing an ostensibly serious article on 'post-modern physics' that was in fact a clever parody. He followed this up with the book *Intellectual Impostures*, jointly authored with Jean Bricmont, which was sharply critical of the work of some of the most fashionable names in the humanities. His motivation, he said in *The Philosophers' Magazine*, had to do with challenging the rise in a 'sloppily thought-out relativism' and with exposing 'the gross abuse of terminology from the natural sciences in the writings of French, American and British authors'.

Sokal is not the only scientist to rail against the shortcomings of the humanities. Twenty-eight years earlier, Peter Medawar had warned in *Science and Literature* that he 'could quote evidence of the beginnings of a whispering campaign against the virtues of clarity. A writer on structuralism in *The Times Literary Supplement* has suggested that thoughts which are confused and tortuous by reason of their profundity are most appropriately expressed in prose that is deliberately unclear. What a preposterously silly idea!' And Richard Dawkins, in a review of *Intellectual Impostures* in the journal *Nature*, encourages people to 'visit the Postmodernism Generator [http://www.cs.monash.edu.au/cgi-bin/postmodern]. It is a literally infinite source of randomly generated, syntactically correct nonsense, distinguishable from the real thing only in being more fun to read … Manuscripts should be submitted to the "Editorial Collective" of *Social Text*, double-spaced and in triplicate.'

Of course, the representatives of the humanities in their turn have not been silent. Derrida is reported to have dismissed Sokal with the words '*le pauvre Sokal*'. Richard Dawkins, in the pages of *Nature*, was accused of failing 'to take the measure of the texts and people he talks about, both those he favours and those he does not'. And Pascal Bruckner, in the *Independent* newspaper, insisted that *Intellectual Impostures* demonstrated the 'total misunderstanding' that exists between Anglo-Saxon culture 'based on facts and information' and French culture 'which depends on interpretation and style'.

It is in the context of these vituperative exchanges that Rée, over the last few years, has published a number of essays and articles, which argue that the 'Science Wars' are based more on misunderstanding than on real disagreements about the status of scientific knowledge. Why, I ask him, is he relatively unmoved by the clash between the purported 'friends' and 'enemies' of science?

'One reason that I am unmoved by the melodrama,' he replies, 'is that historically people have had absolutely no problem with the idea that science is a social phenomenon. Scientists such as J. G. Crowther and J. B. S. Haldane were very keen on the idea that science was the product of various kinds of social relations and that these were the social relations that made it possible to produce knowledge that was testable and reliable. They celebrated historical studies of science as ways of explaining the heroic progress of science towards truth. Now if you imagine yourself back in that situation, then you are reminded that there is not necessarily a conflict between social studies of science and a belief in the truth content of science.'

However, Rée has one caveat. 'It seems to me that these scientists, who thought there was no conflict between science and history, had a notion of scientific progress that I think was superficial – one that nobody really ought to believe anymore. Their model suggested that there was a pre-ordained destination which scientific enquiry was going to end up at. But I think that one can have a very strong idea of scientific progress, without supposing that it is predetermined what is going to be the better form of knowledge that emerges. So my notion is that there are lots of possible ways in which science could progress in the twenty-first century, all of them would be progress, but none of them would be the only possible way in which progress could be made.'

The importance of this caveat is that it is suggestive of an antirealist strand in Rée's thought. Particularly, it seems that in his conception, the progress of science is not governed by the nature of the objects of scientific enquiry. However, a critic might respond that while indeed it is impossible to predict how science will progress, it is nevertheless the case that its progression will be constrained by the nature of the objects it investigates. And moreover, that there are certain ways of looking at the world, certain theories, that are effectively dead, for example, Lamarckism – the belief that it is possible to inherit acquired characteristics. I asked Rée whether this was a point that he would accept and if so whether he felt there was, therefore, no contradiction at all between the objectivity of scientific truth claims and the fact that science is a social and historical phenomenon.

'Yes, I think that I would accept these points,' he replies. 'But one of my proposals for advancing this debate is that there should be an embargo both on the word "objective" and on the word "relativism". I mean it's ludicrous to think that adding the word "objective" makes a truth any more true. There is a very important distinction between propositions that are true and propositions that are false. But I don't know what further distinction is intended by adding the word "objective". It is simply a rhetorical move that does mischief to the whole debate. What people need to understand is that the only truths that are available to us are those of specific historical contexts, but that they are no less true for that.'

In a sociological sense, the claim that truths are necessarily historical is unproblematic. However, it does raise the question as to the criteria for assessing truth-claims. I ask Rée whether he has any settled thoughts on what these are.

'I don't think,' Rée says, 'that there is a useful general answer to that. I mean there are textbook distinctions between correspondence, coherence and pragmatism, that kind of thing, but it doesn't seem to me that these add up to very much. I think you need to ask in more detail about how particular communities work out methods for attaining the kinds of true propositions that they want to get agreement on.'

The problem with this kind of answer is that the absence of general criteria for assessing truth-claims does seem to suggest the kinds of relativism that scientists find so infuriating. If the claim is that both truths and the criteria for truth are constituted in particular discourses, then, without adding in some extra ingredient, how is it possible to distinguish true propositions from false propositions?

'Well,' responds Rée, 'I suppose I should first say that one should always be cautious before deciding that something is false. It is necessary to establish conversations with people who believe seemingly false propositions to determine exactly what it is they believe, then, once you've understood it, you may well find that there is something true in their belief. I think one of the side-effects of getting worked up about the idea of objective truth is that people do tend to get too impatient to investigate the possibility that there may be something they can learn from things that they are at first appalled by. But, of course, that is not to say that there are not some beliefs that are completely false.'

But again, if the criteria for truth are themselves constituted within discourse, what is it that enables us to privilege certain of these criteria so that we can meaningfully say that some beliefs *are* completely false?

'I think this is why Rorty, who is quite wise about this matter, says that you should talk about intersubjectivity rather than objectivity,' replies Rée. 'The question is not about different realities and how they connect up, but different conceptions, different vocabularies, and how they connect up. What you need to do is to experiment with trying to have conversations with people and to see whether you can negotiate some kind of linkage between the way that you're talking about things and the way that they do. To the extent that this strategy is unsatisfactory, it is because our epistemological condition is unsatisfactory. I mean the fact is that it can always turn out that the things that we are convinced are unrevisably true might in fact be problematic in completely unexpected ways.

'I said that there are two terms that should be embargoed,' continues Rée, 'the second one being "relativism". It does seem to me that people who put themselves forward as friends of science, use the word "relativism" to describe a position that they regard as being totally opposed to the notion that there can be such a thing as scientific progress. But if that is what relativism is, then I don't know anyone that believes in it. An alternative tactic is to say "sure, we should all be relativists", because it seems to me that when we actually think about what the term relativism means, then it is a theory about how you get truth and how you know you've got it. And it is simply an unfair debating point to suggest that to be a relativist is to be someone who does not believe there is such a thing as truth. It is just that a relativist is someone who tries to be explicit about the various standards by which truth is measured in different contexts.'

All this seems perfectly reasonable. It is, of course, important that people who make conflicting truth-claims should attempt to establish points of connection in order to examine their respective beliefs and belief systems more closely. It is also at least arguable that scientific truths are by their very nature provisional. And further, it is the case that truths are constructed within particular discourses, and, in that sense at least, they are contextual. But a nagging doubt remains. And it is the same point as before. If the validity of truth-claims can *only* be established in terms of criteria that are themselves internal to particular discourses, what happens when a person inhabiting a non-scientific discourse refuses to accept, despite all attempts at persuasion, some of the established truths of science – for example, that the earth is more than 6,000 years old or that it is not flat? It seems that the logic of the kind of position outlined by Rée means that it is not possible to privilege the scientific version of truth over the non-scientific version. But surely he cannot be happy with that outcome?

'Well, the truth is,' Rée admits, pausing, 'that I'm not really able to give an interesting answer to the question, as you pose it. But I wonder why you put it in terms of beliefs that are so barmy that they are scarcely intelligible? What if it were in terms of something like Holocaust denial, where there is a genuine disagreement and it's not really a disagreement over criteria. It seems to me that while it is undeniably exasperating to find people who stubbornly refuse to accept what you take to be pretty conclusive evidence, it is not fair to be asked "What are you going to do about the fact that you can't change their minds?" – at some point you just have to shrug your shoulders and simply say "Well, I can't."'

But there *are* reasons for posing the question in terms of 'barmy' beliefs. Firstly, plenty of people believe things which in scientific terms are very bizarre – for example, opinion poll data suggests that about a third of Americans reject the idea of human evolution, and another third are undecided. And secondly, the more bizarre the beliefs, the more it becomes clear what is at stake in committing oneself to a conception which holds that the criteria for truth are only internal to particular discourses. Specifically, it brings into sharp focus the fact that this conception allows no definitive grounds for rejecting propositions that we nevertheless are certain are false. So I ask Rée what exactly he would say to someone who insisted that the earth was flat or that mermaids lived under the sea?

'What you have to say is that, as far as I can see – and I may always be wrong – these beliefs are barmy. I think that the phenomenon that you are pointing to is just the fact that people can get into disagreements where it is extremely difficult to make any progress. But I think that that is just our shared epistemological condition, and I don't see that claiming that what you've got is absolute truth and what they have got is not, is going to help. I would use the example of barmy beliefs as a way to bring you round to my slogan, which is: "Neither a realist nor an anti-realist be."

'Listen,' Rée goes on, 'everything that the "friends of science" want to say about the extraordinary achievements and progress of the natural sciences, both in terms of knowledge and in terms of technique, all of these things can be said by someone who describes themselves as a "relativist" and there is no intelligible sense of relativism that would lead you to deny the reality of scientific progress.'

So what then about the ultimate structure of the external world?

Does the contextual nature of all truth-claims mean that this structure is always beyond our reach?

'Well,' says Rée, 'I don't think there is anything more satisfactory than invoking the Rorty move that I have already mentioned. This consists in saying that there is no real difference between talking in an upbeat way about getting to know more about the ultimate structure of the world, and talking in a more depressed kind of way about the possibilities of including more people in a conversation. It seems to me that they really come to the same thing. So the question becomes: how do the particular discourses of specialized sciences relate to other scientific discourses and to discourses outside science?

'If you're in a conversation with someone who is worried about having the ultimate structure of the world taken away from them, then you need to make them see that what they're asking for is beyond what any possible agreement in the future about how to look at the world can deliver. They keep saying that they want objectivity, but they don't actually need it, so the point is to close the gap and to say "you're worried about being deprived of something that actually you haven't got, and you wouldn't know if you had". It's a chimera, this thing that they're worried about having taken away from them.

'Imagine that we're talking with a scientist,' Rée continues, 'worried about his work not being taken seriously – I think that we're paying all the respect that a scientist could dream that we'd pay to the scientific enterprise if we say that, relative to human discourses, science improves the knowledge and control we have over things that matter to us. Of course, you can say "well, it does that because it tells us the truth about the objective structure of the world" – and that's fine, you can say that, but it's hardly an ontological big deal.'

But if that is what Rée thinks is going on in scientific discourses, that they are telling us truths about the objective structure of the world, then surely that is a realist position, it is not some kind of half-way house position?

'Yes,' admits Rée, 'that is what I'm saying, except that I think the word objective is a waste of space. Or are you trying to contrast the objective structure of the world with its subjective structure? I wouldn't if I were you. But rather than "neither a realist nor an anti-realist be", perhaps I should say, "neither an anti-realist nor an anti anti-realist be"!'

Selected Bibliography

'Rorty's Nation', *Radical Philosophy*, no. 87, Jan/Feb 1998

VI Language

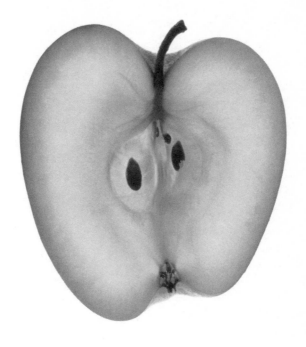

20 Language Matters

Simon Blackburn

A young British philosopher, about to complete a PhD and fantasizing about a glorious career to come, might wish to achieve a number of things. Becoming an Oxford don would not seem too ambitious, and a professorship in the United States followed by another at Cambridge would surely be reasonable a little further down the line. One might hope to edit an academic journal, so why not become editor of *Mind*, the most prestigious of them all? Writing a textbook or two would also be a good idea, so why not one that becomes the standard text for at least a couple of decades? Of course, some serious books would be in order to sit alongside an exemplary series of journal papers. And to cap it all off, a couple of popular bestsellers could be thrown in for good measure.

Many dream such dreams. Simon Blackburn has lived them all. His serious philosophical books include *Essays in Quasi-Realism* and *Ruling Passions*, which grapple with the heavyweight topics of metaphysics and morals. His bestsellers are *Think* and *Being Good*, introductions to general and moral philosophy respectively. Thanks to the clarity and lightness of Blackburn's writing and helped by some beautiful design, they have made Blackburn's name outside of academia.

Blackburn the master philosopher and Blackburn the skilled writer are most perfectly united in his textbooks. His *Oxford Dictionary of Philosophy* showed the breadth of his learning. But arguably his greatest pedagogical achievement is *Spreading the Word*. Lewis

Carroll's White Queen boasted to Alice that she could believe six impossible things before breakfast. We are not told whether one of those was that she could make the canon of the philosophy of language both interesting and accessible, but many would say this fits the bill handsomely.

Blackburn must have had a white queen moment when he decided to write *Spreading the Word*. It remains a favourite of countless teachers and students, and while not as entertaining as Alice's adventures through the looking glass, it does go a long way to making a dry and obscure subject interesting and engaging to the outsider. It was also responsible for introducing several phrases and images well-loved of students and teachers, such as the 'elephant-or-regress' problem; 'bent predicates' and 'wooden communities': language as an orchestra without conductor or score. The decision to use such vivid expressions and images was self-conscious, but also, as Blackburn explains, 'it's partly the way I think and teach. I've always found it easier to have concrete examples or an image, something that focuses one's thoughts. I'm like Berkeley – I'm uncomfortable with abstraction.' However, it is not the manner of Blackburn's writing which makes the philosophy of language interesting.

'One of the reasons it can be interesting,' he explains, 'is that a lot of what's called the philosophy of language is actually philosophy of mind, or philosophy of metaphysics, or philosophy of truth. It's not actually confined to language in the sense that a lexicographer studies language – it's language as used, and then there's not a firm distinction between talking about the language with which we talk about minds, and minds.'

But the subject isn't only of interest to other branches of philosophy. It has much broader implications. 'If you start getting sceptical about language, then all hell breaks loose. The whole "ism" of post-modernism could be seen as a kind of celebration of scepticism about determinate meanings.'

This is the kind of scepticism that maintains that we can never be sure that we mean the same thing by our words as other people do.

If this is true, then we might all be talking at cross-purposes. It also problematizes the notion of truth, since how are we to judge whether what you say is true when we can't even be sure what you mean?

The philosophical issue at the core of this has to do with the way in which using words correctly is a form of rule-following. 'The problem that I think Kripke correctly identified had been raised by the later Wittgenstein,' explains Blackburn. 'If I give you a certain amount of learning time, say, an hour, with this mathematical function, what ensures, if anything, that at the end of the day when you say "now I've got it" and somebody else says "now I've got it" that you've got the same rule? Why shouldn't you take the explanations to introduce one rule, which diverges later on from how the other one takes the rule? If nothing ensures that, what are you then to make of the correctness of future applications?'

In Blackburn's view, this is one of the most pressing issues in the philosophy of language today. 'I think it's a war you can't allow the sceptic to win.'

One curious feature of the philosophy of language is that its importance in twentieth-century Anglo-American philosophy is in inverse proportion to its interest to the wider world. Philosophers arguing about the meaning of 'meaning' are the archetype of the detached academic. So how did the 'linguistic turn' in philosophy come about? Why was the twentieth century the century of the philosophy of language?

'As to why it happened when it did, I'm not sure,' admits Blackburn. 'Those historical questions are always difficult. I think there's a much older strand in philosophy of concentrating on language, and you could argue that Plato, Berkeley and many nineteenth-century writers, such as Bentham, made very significant contributions to the philosophy of language. So I think there's been a slight tendency to exaggerate the degree of that turn. It's a perennial in philosophy for some philosophers to have thought that what's letting us down here are words, our grasp of our words and our understanding of our words. If we can only get that straight then things will get straighter. So I would put a small question mark over the kind of history which says it all started with Frege in 1879. Some people like Michael Dummett say that it's like a chasm separating what happened after and what happened before. I personally would not see it like that.'

Despite these reservations about how the linguistic turn is conceived, Blackburn is the first to agree that, at the very least, the philosophy of language became foregrounded in the last century. Blackburn thinks this has something to do with a kind of optimism that surrounded work in this field from Frege onwards. Many philosophers thought that they were on the verge of replacing 'old-fashioned woolly metaphysics' with a rigorous, formalized philosophy that had at its core a logically perfect language, shorn of the vagaries of ordinary discourse. Once we translated philosophical problems from ordinary language into this purified language of logic, the solutions to philosophical issues would follow as surely as night follows day.

But as Blackburn notes, 'that optimism only lasted until roughly the Second World War'. So the real puzzle is not how the philosophy of language got to occupy centre-stage in the first part of the last century, it's how it remained there during the second, when scepticism about the determinacy of meaning came to the fore, through people like Quine, Wittgenstein and Sellars.

Perhaps one reason why the concerns remained is that once you take seriously the idea that you've got to be clear about what words mean before you can do philosophy, you seem to need to give some answer to the philosophical questions surrounding language before you can get on with the rest of philosophy.

'It could seem that way,' says Blackburn, 'and I do think that's a self-image that certain analytic philosophers, certainly ones that have concentrated on meaning, sometimes have. You know, the honest under-labourer who's clearing away the intellectual rubbish that's hampering understanding. My own sense is that there's something false about that self-image. First off, if you look at the other enterprises that try and advance understanding, whether it's science, history or whatever it might be, they don't seem hampered by the lack of a good philosophy of language – they just go on and do it. So the idea that we philosophers come along with our sort of mine-clearing equipment so that others can walk over the field, that just doesn't seem to be right.'

What's more, plenty of good philosophy has been done without any final answers being reached in the philosophy of language.

'That's right. To be fair, it's got to be said that the optimistic self-image of philosophy of language started to look quite sickly in the last twenty years, and the centre of gravity has shifted to the philosophy of mind.'

So a major problem remains unsolved in the philosophy of language. How do we navigate between the Scylla of language as a fully determinate, quasi-scientific system of which we can give a fully formalized account, and the Charybdis of language as an entirely indeterminate, 'anything goes' post-modern mélange?

'I think that's a major philosophical problem,' says Blackburn. 'I do navigate between them but I don't think anybody's solved it.' Blackburn talks about the 'holistic blancmange' we've been left with. 'If that's what the language is then it's very hard to see yourself as a creation of reason, a creature following rational pathways to getting rationally supported conclusions, and you do get the post-modern scepticism that it's all a matter of persuasion and there's no distinction between rhetoric and investigation. I think we've retreated from that extreme scepticism but I don't think there's a philosophy of language that tells you how, or where to start. So that's a big challenge facing the subject.'

One problem is perhaps that many philosophers try to give an analysis of what meaning is in terms of a precise formula, but as soon as you start thinking about how varied and rich language is, that immediately seems hopeless. Maybe we need a more piecemeal approach to the problems, addressing issues such as meaning and representation individually, not as part of one, whole, philosophy of language.

'I think there's something in that,' agrees Blackburn. 'Look at the big successes that you can chalk up in the philosophy of language. You've got the theory of descriptions, which is a very particular kind of phenomenon that Russell picked on, so that was a very constrained success, although it was thought of as a paradigm of philosophy all round. If you think again of Austin and *How To Do Things With Words*, again Austin looked at what you can do with language, again very successfully. And then of course you might think of someone like Chomsky highlighting the way in which we have this extensive linguistic repertoire out of a finite, rather restricted starting point. So there have been a number of insights and developments that we've had and they've always been in a sense rather particular. One of the frustrating things about the philosophy of language is that individually they haven't brought us any nearer to understanding what's distinctive about ourselves as language users. There's something interesting about that. You may be right. It may be because at that level of generality there's nothing interesting to say.'

One of the most helpful features of *Spreading the Word* comes at the very beginning, where Blackburn presents a triangle with speakers, language and the world at each of its points. This simple diagram helps to make a lot of sense of the place of the philosophy of language.

'The initial use that I made of that diagram,' explains Blackburn, 'is to point out three different starting places for philosophy. You might say the first thing to do is to understand ourselves, as Hume does, for example; you might say the first thing you've got to do then is understand our language, and so do the philosophy of language; or you might think, no, what you've got to do is settle the nature of the world, the things that surround us and after that our own nature and the nature of language will fall out. That in a sense is the scientific approach – the rest is stamp collecting. So that was the initial point.'

Blackburn also makes use of the triangle to explain a methodological issue at the heart of the subject. 'Our aim is to understand all three poles of that triangle. The methodological crux is where you start, whether you're obsessed by word-to-world relations or people-to-people relations.'

The diagram illustrates how the particular preoccupations of one's time are not perennial, and also how to relate it to other approaches in other times which may seem very different.

'I think that's right,' says Blackburn. 'Unless you have a generous conception of what might be bothering somebody, you get this really quite terribly biased and in a sense provincial approach to the history of philosophy. Famously some people seem to have thought that someone like Locke or Hume was really intending to write a late twentieth-century paper for *Analysis* – they were just doing it terribly badly. Of course, that's ridiculous.'

As someone who has tried to make the philosophy of language as plain as possible, Blackburn has no truck with those who claim the obscurity of some of its writings is an inevitable result of the subject's difficulty.

'It is difficult and its fine practitioners tend to write very difficult papers, sometimes technically difficult. But I think its difficulties were compounded by a certain pride in its difficulty.'

We won't name names, but astute readers of this book may be able to identify the philosopher who Blackburn says 'is not notorious for getting his prose into its clearest, most lucid and shortest form. Kant famously says of his own writing that there are books which couldn't be so clear had they not been so long. I think that's a neat shelter.' But he is quick to praise those who have written well on the subject, specifically Russell, Ryle and Austin.

However, Blackburn also says that one reason why philosophy can appear irrelevant is that academics work on the minutiae of arguments, and then relating this back to issues of general concern becomes difficult.

'I think that's probably characteristic of almost all human

enquiry,' he says. 'Take some research in social science, for example. Psychologists discover that men are unfaithful sometimes, and you wonder how grown men can spend their time on that. But of course often it's because some detailed statistic had been waiting in connection with some kind of research programme.

'There's no question that the style of analytic philosophy, especially philosophy of language, did lead to minutiae coming to the fore. It's a difficult call, I think, whether those minutiae connected sufficiently to the wider intellectual pursuit to justify the attention they used to be paid.'

Blackburn has published two books aimed at a general readership. *Think* is a general introduction to philosophy and *Being Good* a short introduction to ethics. Since *Spreading the Word* tried to show the wider significance of philosophy of language for philosophy, and these books try to show the wider significance of philosophy for normal life, is it possible to cut out the middle man and consider what the wider significance of the philosophy of language is for the average person on the street?

'Hume said that the philosopher lives remote from business, and that's true,' replies Blackburn. 'I can't go out and claim that by reading Austin you will gain such and such benefits in your everyday life. That's not the way it works. As I say in the introduction to *Think*, I think that you can take a high ground or more pragmatic grounds with these things. The high ground has got to be just that it's one of the world's great literatures. If you're ignorant of Aristotle, Hume and Wittgenstein it's like being ignorant of Shakespeare, Jane Austen or George Eliot and this ought to be regarded as shameful in the same way as ignorance of great literature would be. A much more interesting, pragmatic ground is that I really do think that unless people have some tools for reflecting on the language they use they're apt to be behaving unselfconsciously, and unreflective behaviour is often behaviour that's at the mercy of forces which we don't understand. So I think that realizing the state of your language is a very important device for realizing the state of your culture at this time in history, and in politics.'

Interestingly, Blackburn does not make a sharp division himself between these introductory texts and his large, academic output.

'It's curious,' he explains. 'I don't make a distinction in my own mind between explaining the subject to myself or other people and contributing to it. Somehow they seem to be seamless. I do write articles that appear in *Mind* and I suppose then I put on a professional hat and don't necessarily write in the same way, but even there it's not sharply divided. I wrote a paper that came out in 1995 called "Practical Tortoise Racing" which is about Lewis Carroll and the tortoise paradox. That was written originally as a piece of comedy for a conference on Lewis Carroll. But it makes a serious point and got into a journal.

'There's a sense in which I wrote *Spreading the Word* for myself, because I had been teaching this stuff for years and didn't think there was a good introductory book at the time. I found myself again and again explaining to students what was going on and I thought it was time to put this down on paper. It was partly an exercise in self-validation – do I really understand this?'

Is the connection between explaining and doing philosophy a product of the fact that in presenting an argument you are forced to formulate it in some way, and in doing so its persuasiveness or flaws become evident?

'And you've got to have your philosophical brain working because if you try and present, for example, Fodor's language of thought, and use an argument against it as a teaching device, then I'd better be sure I've got it right. So then you're philosophizing.'

I'm reminded of something John Searle said in an interview: 'If you can't say it clearly you don't understand it yourself.'

'I think that's right,' says Blackburn. 'I was picked up by Bernard Williams, perhaps rightly, for quoting in the introduction to *Spreading the Word* Quintilian, who said "do not write so that you can be understood, but so that you cannot be misunderstood". Williams

snapped at that and said it was an impossible ideal. You can always
be misunderstood, and of course he's right. But I think the point of
Quintilian's remark isn't 'write so as to avoid any possible
misunderstanding' but to remember that it's difficult and that it's
your job to make it as easy as you can.'

Philosophers of language, take note.

Selected Bibliography

Spreading the Word (Oxford: Oxford University Press, 1984)
Oxford Dictionary of Philosophy (Oxford: Oxford University Press, 1994)
Ruling Passions (Oxford: Oxford University Press, 1998)
Think (Oxford: Oxford University Press, 1999)
Being Good (Oxford: Oxford University Press, 2001)

21 Truth and Meaning

Michael Dummett

British philosophy in the twentieth century had several characteristics which did not help endear it to the wider public. Analytic philosophy, as the dominant tradition was called, was difficult and removed from the interests of everyday life. Owing its origins to the work of Frege, Russell and Whitehead, it dealt with technical issues concerning mathematics, logic and meaning. Not only are these questions difficult for the uninitiated to find interesting, they were usually written about in a style which was impenetrable to non-philosophers. At the very least a grasp of basic symbolic logic was required. The effect was to make philosophy seem remote, technical, difficult and boring.

In a parallel universe where everyone was excited by the concerns of analytic philosophy, Professor Sir Michael Dummett would be a superstar. His specializations match exactly the description given above of remote, technical, difficult and – for some – boring analytic philosophy. Dummett himself is none of these things. In person, he is neither difficult nor boring. This genial, frail, chain-smoking septuagenarian is an agreeable, good-humoured conversationalist, who frequently punctuates proceedings with hearty, coughy chuckles. Nor is he remote from the concerns of everyday life, being a long-time and tireless campaigner and activist for the rights of refugees. But there's no getting away from the fact that the philosophical writings of Dummett are difficult, or from the uncharitable question, whether it's the philosophical or the writing part that makes reading him such a labour.

To make sense of Dummett's work, one has to get some kind of grasp of the project that lies behind it. First of all, it's important to recognize that, more often than not, Dummett is exploring ideas, suggesting ways forward, rather than advancing a finished product. In his valedictory lecture, he noted that his aims are 'frustrated when it is mistaken as the advocacy of a large and sharply defined philosophy'.

'I think that's about right,' agrees Dummett, when confronted with this characterization of his output. 'It used to be that philosophers were expected to produce a system. That was well known in Germany. Each professor had his system which students were expected to study and accept. There's a fine story I heard about a man called Salmon who gave a very interesting talk about Husserl on the radio, decades ago. He was a man who had spent a large part of his life studying philosophy. So far as I know, he never produced any. He studied at Oxford, Paris and finally in Freiburg under Husserl. He described arriving at Husserl's house and presenting himself as Husserl's new student. Husserl answered the door himself, asked him to wait, went back into the house and came back carrying a pile of books and he said, "Hier sind meine Werke" [here are my works]. The student was expected to go away and read them all before he came back. Well I rather disapprove of that tradition.

'Russell, of course, did have a philosophical system at various points of his life, but he kept changing it. That's better.'

This lack of a 'philosophy of Michael Dummett' is particularly pertinent in his writings on realism – the question of whether or not there is a knowable reality independent of our experience. 'I wanted to explore what I called anti-realism or what I now call justification-ism as an alternative to realism,' he recalls. 'I've explored what it is to be an anti-realist, not so much because I wanted to adopt that as my philosophy, although at certain times I felt very strongly inclined to do so. But not mainly for that reason. Mainly it was for the reason that I wanted to make sure whether it was a viable position, what the consequences of it were going to be, both within the philosophy of language and within metaphysics.'

The question of realism may seem removed from the theme of language and meaning, but Dummett says: 'It's obvious to me that the philosophy of language and metaphysics come very close together.' As with the works of Hilary Putnam, it is impossible with Dummett to see where his philosophy of language ends and his metaphysics begins.

'The notion of truth is the point at which the theory of meaning is linked to metaphysics,' explains Dummett. 'Different theories of meaning, different conceptions of meaning, go with different conceptions of truth. Practically everybody realizes that the notions of meaning and of truth are very closely linked, that's why there are constantly books written with "truth and meaning" or "meaning and truth" in their titles.'

Dummett illustrates the link with Wittgenstein's quote at the start of the *Tractatus* in which he says the world is constituted by what facts obtain, not what things are in it.

'Facts are true propositions,' explains Dummett, 'you can't have the notion of a fact without a notion of the truth. And what conception of truth you have depends on what, in a very large way, propositions you think are true. For example, the facts recognized by people who think there's no truth in future-tense statements, are different from the facts recognized by people who think the future is just as determinate as the past. So that's where the link comes, between the theory of meaning and metaphysics.'

Some have argued that the concept of 'truth' is unanalysable, that it is a kind of 'primitive concept' that defies definition in terms of other, clearer or simpler concepts. Dummett rejects this possibility.

'I don't think "truth" is a primitive notion. I don't think there can be an explanation of the notion of truth which is going to satisfy everyone, whatever conception of meaning you have. Different conceptions of meaning have a different conception of truth. So I think given a particular conception, you can explain relative to that view what truth is, but you can't find an explanation that will satisfy everyone.'

What Dummett is saying is that because the notions of truth and meaning are so connected, the meaning of 'truth' has to be relative to the theory of meaning which you adopt, and that means it can't be a primitive notion because a primitive notion would not depend on which theory of meaning you adopt.

One can see from this exchange some of the reasons why Dummett is not easy to read. When one is very much exploring a terrain which has so many unclear borders between related territories, it is easy to get lost. Perhaps one way to keep one's bearings is to think of Dummett's work as an attempt to define the right distinctions and concepts that need to be used to talk about language. Although this is in some ways a crude caricature of both Dummett and the analytic tradition within which he works, it does provide a sort of compass to guide us as we read him.

Take, for instance, the starting point of much of Dummett's work, the philosophy of Gottlob Frege. Frege introduced the distinction between sense and reference in meaning. Put crudely, the reference of a word or utterance is the thing it stands for, and the sense is how we conceive of it, how we understand it.

The problem is, it just isn't that easy. This is what happens when you ask Dummett to explain how he understands reference. If this is unfamiliar, you are advised to go slowly; bear with it and it will make sense.

'The notion of reference – *Bedeutung* in Frege's ill-chosen term – seems to me to be exactly in effect that of semantic value. That is to say, semantic theory is a theory about the determination as true or otherwise of sentences in accordance with their composition out of words and phrases; and the semantic value of a constituent of a sentence is that by which it contributes to determining the truth or otherwise of the whole sentence. That is why Frege takes it for granted that anything that really contributes to determining the truth or falsity of a sentence must have a *Bedeutung*, must have some semantic value. So I think it's quite wrong to think, although he often used language which would tempt one into believing it, that he

thought that everything was a kind of name and stood in relation to some element of reality as a name stands to its bearer. I think that's a complete misunderstanding of the whole notion.'

Having got 'reference' straight, let's move on to 'sense'.

'What Frege came to realize very clearly was that you can't explain just in terms of that notion – the notion of semantic value, the notion that is needed for a semantic theory – what an understanding of a sentence is, a grasp of the thought expressed by the sentence. You can most easily explain that by quoting Kant. Kant said that every object is given to us in a particular way. We don't have contact with the object as such. We conceive of it in a particular way, or perceive it in a particular way. I think that Frege essentially generalized that. Not only every object, but every property, every relation is given to us in a particular way. When you're concerned with just the semantic theory, then the object is all you want, because once you fix the object that a singular term denotes, you've exhausted its contribution to determining the truth-value of the whole. But you haven't explained how we conceive of the object, how we understand the term that refers to the object, so that is the essence of that distinction.'

This is Dummett speaking rather than writing, so it might be thought that things become clearer on the printed page. But here's a fairly random quote from one of Dummett's published papers:

'For Frege, the reference of an expression is an extra-linguistic entity, and in the informal semantics, or model theory, which has been developed from his ideas, an interpretation associates with each individual constant, predicate etc., of the language a non-linguistic entity of a suitable type.'

Clearly, we're in deep philosophical waters here. This interview really is trying to throw you a lifejacket, not push you under.

Perhaps because it seems at first so simple and then gets so horribly complex, the distinction between sense and reference is one of the more difficult parts of Dummett's work of trying to carve up the anatomy of language accurately. Some other distinctions are more amenable to understanding. For example, Dummett follows Frege in distinguishing between the sentence and the thought, where the thought is not identical to any given sentence which expresses it.

'A thought, which is what other philosophers call a proposition,' explains Dummett, 'is something that must for Frege be true or false. It's not true for you and false for me, it's not true at one time and false at another time. Then, of course, from time to time, he mentions things that would tempt you to say that it's true at one time and false at another. Those are sentences which contain indexical elements: "it's very cold *today*" and so on. So he says rather vaguely, when such sentences are uttered, the sentence itself does not suffice to express the thought. The time of utterance, for example, enters into the expression of the thought. This is a rather vague account of all that. I think that it's also inadequate.'

Dummett sees part of the difficulty in working out how we determine what the thought is, given that many utterances which express a thought are ambiguous. 'There's an excellent example, I first read it in Putnam, but it was taken from David Lewis, about the word "flat",' he continues. 'It depends on the context how flat a thing has to be to be rightly called flat. Driving along you could say the country is very flat, but that doesn't mean that there's no variation in it. On the other hand, if it's a billiard table, there have got to be pretty exacting standards. With all these things, we judge what someone meant from all sorts of indications, including what he is likely to have meant, what he is likely to have been saying, and I think there's no way in which it is possible to circumscribe the context in such a way that it will determine a unique interpretation. The interpretation is a matter of selecting what thought, in Frege's sense, a person was expressing or was asserting to be true. And so it determines the conditions for truth. But I think the fact that there is no way of laying down exact rules for what interpretation is to be adopted, that is a strong motive for saying that truth attaches to thoughts or propositions and not to sentences.'

Readers who think this all sounds rather uninteresting may be surprised to learn that Dummett agrees. 'I think the argument whether truth is to be attributed to thoughts or sentences is a sterile one, because if you're concerned with a theory of meaning, you've got to have something which attaches to sentences – you're trying to explain the meaning of sentences, so you've got to talk about sentences. But all the theory of meaning can do is to show the range of possible interpretations. How you select the right interpretation, that is something that no systematic theory can do.'

The distinction between a thought and any particular utterance or sentence that expresses it may appear to be straightforward. But if you accept the distinction and also maintain, as Dummett does, that 'thoughts are of their essence communicable', then there is a puzzle. There is no problem with the idea that sentences or utterances are communicable, since language is a public medium. But if thoughts and sentences are not identical, and thoughts are essentially private, doesn't that make the idea of the essential communicability of thoughts problematic?

'No, I don't think so,' says Dummett. 'To start with, in actual conversations, such as we're having now, if I put, as people sometimes do, the wrong interpretation on what you said, unintended, that you didn't intend, and that becomes clear from my response, you can explain. Of course, it's more difficult with writing, but I think that Frege dreamt of a perfect language in which such difficulties could never arise. There'd be no ambiguity, no vagueness, no need for any interpretation. Well that's a dream. We don't have such a language and I don't think we could have such a language. But that doesn't inhibit the communication of thoughts. It just requires communication to be something which engages the intelligence of the hearer as well as of the speaker.

'Words are very flexible things. Put together they lose a good deal of that flexibility, but not completely, not so much as to rule out some of the necessity of interpretation. I'm not using "interpretation" in the way that Davidson does. For Davidson, the hearer's interpretation is constructing a whole theory of meaning for the speaker, selecting between the possible interpretations, the inter-pretations which language leaves us to do on the basis of probability and so on. That's not at all what I mean. He would be very silly if he were saying that, you realize. You do so without thinking, you rule out interpretations which would make someone else's remarks just silly.'

This is a kind of 'transcendental argument': an argument that starts from the facts of experience and shows what must be true for these experiences to be possible. In this case, the argument proceeds from the fact that we are able, in conversation and in writing, to notice that we've given the wrong interpretation or misread the thought expressed in the words the person has said, to the conclusion that communicating thoughts must be possible. It shows that there is both a distinction between the thought and the particular sentence and also that the thought is nevertheless communicable.

'Yes,' Dummett agrees, before going on to chew over some of the idea's repercussions. 'The other day, I was struck very much by how much my own thinking has been formed by Frege, when I was reading a review in the *European Journal of Philosophy*. It praised the author for rejecting what he called the thought–language link, or some such thing. This author was maintaining that you could have thoughts without concepts, not just unverbalized thoughts but ones which couldn't be expressed in language because they didn't involve concepts. On reflection I still think this is an idiotic idea, but I was immediately brought up short by this because I was, as it were, brought up by Frege. He was a kind of tutor to me, and for him, what this man meant by "concepts" was what Frege meant by "sense", and senses are thought-constituents. Thoughts are essentially complex. I can't see how you can have a thought which is not complex, and what it is composed of are senses. You can think that much without thinking of senses as senses of words or expressions.

'Frege went further and thought that we can't have thoughts

Selected Bibliography

Frege: Philosophy of Language (London: Duckworth, 1973)

Truth and Other Enigmas (London: Duckworth, 1978)

Frege and Other Philosophers (Oxford: Clarendon Press, 1991)

Origins of Analytical Philosophy (Cambridge, MA: Harvard University Press, 1994)

On Immigration and Refugees (London: Routledge, 2001)

22 Out of our Heads

'I make no secret of changing my mind on one or two important issues.' It's a pretty unexceptional admission, but for the speaker of these words the issue of changing one's mind has a peculiar force. Hilary Putnam has written on a wide range of topics, encompassing metaphysics, the philosophy of language, and the philosophy of mind. He has spearheaded several of twentieth-century philosophy's most powerful movements. Putnam was the founding father of functionalism – the position that mental states are computational states, a position he has since repudiated. He is also responsible for one of recent philosophy's few memorable sound-bites: 'Cut the pie any way you like, "meanings" just ain't in the *head*!' from his seminal paper 'The Meaning of "Meaning"'. This encapsulated the theory of semantic externalism, of which more later.

His work has thus become essential reading for anyone serious about contemporary debate in all these areas. Yet still some know him best for changing his mind.

It's something that baffles Putnam, who can reel off a long list of books and papers he wrote a quarter of a century ago which he still stands by. He also points to colleagues, like Jerry Fodor, who have made some pretty big U-turns themselves without being saddled with a reputation for inconstancy.

Fixating on this aspect of Putnam's work is misplaced for two reasons. First of all, not changing one's mind is hardly a virtue in itself. 'I've never thought it a virtue to adopt a position and try to get famous as a person who defends that position,' says Putnam, 'like a purveyor of a brand name, or someone selling cornflakes.' Putnam recalls Carnap, with whom he worked at Princeton for a year. 'I remember how often he said "I used to think so and so; I *now* think so and so". I remember admiring that very much.'

More important, however, is that readers who focus too much on where Putnam has changed his mind are in danger of missing the constants. Putnam himself says, 'Much of the apparatus that I depend on in my own reasoning has not changed.' This apparatus is most evident when one looks at the backbone of his philosophy which comprises his work on language and meaning.

Putnam's philosophy of language rests on two key claims, known as semantic externalism and semantic holism. The former is most closely associated with him and is summed up in the 'cut the pie' line. Just what does semantic externalism add up to?

'I would say that to be an externalist about meaning is to say that the world external to the brain or mind plays a much bigger part in deciding what our words mean than the tradition emphasizes. For example, the fact that there is only one liquid that looks like water and freezes at anywhere near that freezing point and boils at anywhere near that boiling point and that satisfies thirst and so on – the fact that the world provides exactly *one* liquid that does all that has a lot to do with fixing what we mean by the word "water". I call that the contribution of the environment.

'The other thing is that philosophers have for a long time philosophized as if language were a tool that one person could use in isolation. I think it's a tool like a battleship or a factory that takes a whole lot of people to use. So as an externalist I can say that I can get by using the word "gold" all right even though I would be pretty unreliable if I were on a desert island and there were pieces of shiny, yellow metal and the question was, are they really gold? I couldn't tell you, but normally I can rely on an expert who can say.'

This second characteristic of semantic externalism is what Putnam calls 'the division of linguistic labour'. Although this is a philosophical thesis, Putnam believes there is a lot of scope for empirical research to flesh out just how this works.

'I said at the beginning and still think that exactly how that works is not something to be settled *a priori*,' he explains. 'People ought to go out and look, and I have had some, not as many as I would like, conversations with anthropologists who find the division of linguistic labour in even the most primitive societies. One example I remember being given by an anthropologist is that in the tribe this anthropologist was working with, men and women had different competences in the use of names for birds. The men who hunt the birds distinguish many more species, which makes perfect sense. Presumably a woman could refer to one of those birds, even though she can't herself identify them, because she can use her husband or some other male hunter as an expert.'

In sum, semantic externalism is about seeing how important facts external to us – such as the way the world actually is and the way the linguistic community works – are in fixing the meanings of words.

The other doctrine concerning language Putnam adheres to is semantic holism. Putnam has a problem with this phrase because, as he puts is, 'One must remember that the term was invented, as far as I know, by an enemy.' That enemy is Michael Dummett, who used the phrase to describe Quine. 'We've sort of at times used it as a badge of honour,' says Putnam.

However, the badge is tarnished by a characterization of semantic holism given by Dummett which Putnam rejects. 'I always have to say that if it were really defined the way Dummett defined it – if it's the view that any change in your beliefs is a change in the meaning of all your words – that is certainly not a view that I've ever held or that Quine, when he allowed himself to talk about meaning, ever held.'

So what is the correct characterization of semantic holism, the one Putnam would agree with? 'We holists say that interpretation is a holistic matter. That is to say, what you reasonably take a word to mean can always be changed when you see more text, more what linguists call 'corpus'. In that sense, no finite amount of corpus – not that the fact the word is used here, and here, and here, and here – can infallibly show what the word means. Unless you know that it's never used in some additional way that you haven't taken account of, you can't rule out the possibility of having to redefine it.

'There are very simple examples of that. Someone who heard a German speaker use the word *Stuhl*, or a French speaker use the word *chaise*, would naturally say, "Oh I see what it means, it exactly means chair." And that's the meaning most dictionaries give. But eventually you will discover, if you're American – I'm not sure about British usage – in American usage an armchair is a chair, but it's not a *chaise* in French, it's a *fauteuil* and it's not a *Stuhl* in German, it's a *Sessel*. That is, I think, a very nice example of the way in which meaning assignments are fallible.

'I think holism always seemed evident to me. One of my three majors in college was in linguistic analysis, it was the first department in the world. In fact, it wasn't even a department, it was a section of the anthropology department run by Zelig Harris and the only other undergraduate I knew in that department was Noam Chomsky, whom I've known ever since high school. So we were the two undergraduates in linguistic analysis in 1944–48 at Penn. Anyone who has seen a corpus from field linguistics knows – I didn't actually go into the field myself, but my senior paper for Harris was on Nahuatl, the Aztec language, and of course, once you work with real corpus then meaning holism is just forced on you. There are some accounts of meaning such as Fodor's, according to which each word has one meaning, a meaning which is fixed by its causal connection with a "property", but that has nothing to do with the way words behave in a real language. So meaning holism seemed to me quite obvious.'

The connection between externalism and holism is the importance to both of contextuality. 'Semantic externalism is one kind of context dependence,' explains Putnam. 'It says that to know the meaning of a word you have to see the context in which it's used, not just the speaker's brain or mental images. That's a kind of contextuality. Meaning holism says that more context can flip the best hypothesis about what a word means. So they're connected by their mutual connection to contextuality, to the fact that the meaning of a word is something that it has, as Frege says, in the context of a sentence, or, as Wittgenstein says in a couple of places, "in the stream of life", which is my favourite context principle. I call it Wittgenstein's context principle.'

Both these views have remained constants in Putnam's thought for over a quarter of a century. But that is not to say his thinking has stood still. In his more recent writing he has put forward the idea that 'meaning is in part a normative notion'. What exactly does this mean?

Putnam expresses doubts about whether the phrase 'meaning is a normative notion' is 'a happy formulation'. Nonetheless, in essence, what Putnam means when he does employ this terminology is, 'What we say a word means or what we mean by a sentence on a given occasion, that's very often a judgement as to what it's most reasonably taken to mean, and that is essentially normative. Although he doesn't use the word "normative", I like very much Charles Travis's book *Unshadowed Thought*. He very often uses the notion of what a reasonable judge would say. That seems to me, even in a very traditional sense, a normative notion.'

The crucial point being made here is that if meaning is normative – that is to say, if it relies to a certain extent on judgement, rather than just 'facts' – several popular theories about meaning are ruled out. For example, Putnam recalls the early 1970s *is*. 'At that time people were very optimistic about characterizing the meaning of words, especially nouns, in terms of what they're causally connected to. There the normativity cuts strongly against that.'

Putnam has a favourite story to illustrate the normativity of meaning, which he borrows from a joke told to him by the great historian of metallurgy, Cyril Stanley Smith.

The joke centres around the notion of phlogiston, a substance once believed to be present in all combustible materials but which has long since passed into the dustbin of chemistry. Putnam recalls Smith joking that 'there *is* such a thing as phlogiston, it's valence electrons. The phenomenon which both phlogiston and oxygen were invoked to explain are phenomena that involve valence electrons. Nevertheless, we do not say that phlogiston is valence electrons, as Smith jokingly "proposed", even though the phenomena which phlogiston was introduced to explain *are* causally connected to valence electrons, we say that there isn't such a thing as phlogiston. That has to do with a normative appraisal of whether it's better to say that the theory was approximately right although mistaken about bla-bla, or to say it's just wrong, there is no such thing. You can't just look at what causes you to use the word. You also have to look at the whole context in which it's used.'

Reading and hearing Putnam talk about such issues, one becomes aware of a general trend in his thought away both from views that treat language and meaning as quasi-scientific phenomena, and from attempts to over-systemize the philosophy of language. There is more scepticism concerning the extent to which one can provide a fully systematic explanation in various aspects of philosophy in Putnam's work as times goes by.

'I don't think meanings are scientific objects,' confirms Putnam. 'There's a big question, then, whether that means that they don't exist. In a sense, that's Quine's conclusion – that we can go on talking about meanings but they don't really exist at all. That leads to a much wider question, whether the world can be described simply using the vocabulary of first-class physics or first-class rigorous science. I don't think it can be, but that's a very large question.'

Once again, at the core of his thinking in these areas is contextuality. In the early part of the twentieth century, the logical positivists, such as Carnap, thought you could have context-independent meanings because, as Putnam puts it, 'there was this privileged class of observation terms – his examples in the last paper he wrote on this were "blue", "touches" and "warmer than" – which had what he called "complete meaning", so that you could explain the meaning of any sentence in the language (if it were formalized à la logical positivism) by in some way relating it to these observation sentences.'

However, the idea of context-independent observation terms has not proven to be very tenable. Putnam cites an example of a counterexample offered by Charles Travis. 'If I go to the stationer and I ask for blue ink and it looks black in the bottle, but I dip my pen in and write and sure enough the text is blue, then I would normally say, yes, he sold me blue ink. I don't care how it looks in the bottle, I care how it looks on the paper. But in another context I might not call it blue ink. It goes back to the whole idea of a sense-datum language and all that. I think we need to rethink what meaning is. I think we expect from logical positivism that the meaning of sentences should exhibit very little context sensitivity. Words like "I" and "this" and the present tense introduce a certain element of context sensitivity, but that's all.

'Now a number of philosophers, like Travis and myself, and Wittgenstein and Austin well before us, would argue that sentences do not normally have context-independent truth conditions. It's the meaning of the sentence or the words plus the context that fixes the truth conditions. We need to rethink what meaning is. That's something I really called for in "The Meaning of Meaning", by the way, where I argue that we need to rethink what a normal form for a dictionary entry for a word should ideally look like.'

However, whereas this proposal calls for more work in linguistics, semantics and lexicography, Putnam bemoans the fact that 'philosophy stands almost entirely apart from that, giving much too much significance to ideal language, mathematical logic and all that.'

Wittgenstein is a figure who seems to be behind a lot of the recent trends in Putnam's work. However, it would be wrong to see Putnam as having become a fully-fledged Wittgensteinian. 'In general, I don't like the limits Wittgenstein puts on philosophy or Wittgensteinians put on philosophy, but many of his criticisms of the traps we fall into seem to me profoundly right. Some of them come from a misplaced belief that systematicity must be possible, what he calls a "philosopher's must". I've also come to appreciate this, as I've grown more aware of the importance of the notion of context sensitivity, I see that now really as running through a lot of Wittgenstein's arguments.'

Where he does stand shoulder to shoulder with Wittgenstein is on the issue of what 'rigorous' philosophy is. 'I think that we gave a certain metaphysical significance – and I am a mathematician too, as well as a philosopher – to mathematical logic in the twentieth century, and I think that was a mistake. I think we still suffer from the idea that formalizing a sentence tells you what it "really" says. Perhaps we're now doing something similar with Chomskian linguistics. We're still suffering from the idea that these formalisms tell us what tightening something up must be like. There I am very much with Wittgenstein. That should not be what tightening up something in philosophy means. In fact, here philosophy is not unique. It happens periodically in sociology, it happens periodically in economics, it happens periodically in all the social sciences, that we get this dream that we can take over formalisms from some exact science and then we will *really* be making progress.'

Oddly enough, Putnam believes part of the attraction of some of these formalisms is their obscurity. 'I think part of the appeal of mathematical logic is that the formulas look mysterious – you write backward Es!'

Another figure for whom Putnam has a long-standing respect is J. L. Austin, whose 'ordinary language' philosophy was enormously influential in postwar Oxford.

'I remember that I decided very early that there are two different theses one has to distinguish. One is that philosophy can and should for the most part be done in ordinary language, about which I agree with Austin enormously. The other is that it's *about* ordinary language, which I don't agree with. I think there's a tendency not to separate those two.

'So, on the one hand, philosophy should be done in ordinary language: when you can't state a philosophical point you're trying to make without a plain violation of ordinary language, that's at least a bad sign. The fact that we never speak of "directly perceiving" and "not directly perceiving" in everyday language in the way that traditional epistemologists do was a sign that something was really quite wrong with the traditional philosophy of perception, something already noticed in the eighteenth century by Thomas Reid, by the way. Reid sounds very Austinian when he fulminates against the strange ways philosophers talk about perception. I think that's a corrective one should apply to one's own thought.

'But on the other hand, if another philosopher uses an expression in an extraordinary way or violates its ordinary use, I would never *immediately* conclude that he or she is talking nonsense. Then the idea of ordinary language becomes a kind of straitjacket – we know what ordinary language is, we know when it's violated and we know that when it's violated nonsense results – I don't accept any one of those three statements.'

Putnam is always interested in seeing the attractions of positions he ultimately rejects. For instance, though he is not now a functionalist, he can see the positions' merits.

'In the end, what I think is that there's an insight in functionalism, you might call it a deontologized Aristotelianism. Insofar as functionalism means that we think of mental states as ways we are organized to relate to the world, that seems to me right. Taking externalism into account, I would have to say, with Gareth Evans, that there are *world-involving* ways of relating to the world, not just ways our brains are structured, but "transactions with the environment", in John Dewey's sense. So I still think there was an insight in functionalism. But the mistake was the idea that you could capture those ways by computer programs. Well, the way I've put it for many years is that you can turn functionalism's argument against the old identity theory of Smart and Place against itself. The argument of functionalism against the old brain–mind identity theory was that a given so-called mental state, such as being in pain, or wanting food, or wondering where's a good place to build a nest – a given mental state can be realized, and is realized, in different organisms in very different physical states. Functionalists like to say that mental states are "compositionally plastic". They can be realized in more than one composition, which means they're not just identical with some physical–chemical property. I would now say, and I think this was anticipated by some of the fathers of computer science, that they are also *computationally* plastic, that mental states can be realized in many *different* computer programs. That's why the whole language of identity, or reduction, was a mistake – it was a nice dream and it had to be tried – the dream was to reduce the predicates of vernacular psychology to predicates of computer science or neurology-cum-computer science. That seems to me to be a dream that doesn't work, but we learnt a lot by trying it.'

On a more personal note, in the introduction to his recent *Renewing Philosophy,* Putnam says that he is a practising Jew. Although the connection may not be obvious, Colin McGinn, in his review of Putnam's *The Threefold Cord*, pays Putnam the back-handed compliment that his fundamental problem is that he cannot bear to be boring.

'That should be the worst thing said about me!' laughs Putnam, whose writing is indeed a welcome antidote to the dry, humourless style of many of his contemporaries. Both the style of writing and the acknowledgement of his religious views reflect something quite important about how Putnam sees philosophy.

'I think that the philosopher should to some extent disclose himself as a human being,' he explains. 'That's something that James argues in Lecture One in *Pragmatism*. I'm paraphrasing him, but he quotes a Walt Whitman line, saying "Who touches this book touches a man." He indicates that that is what he wants people to say about his book. That seems right to me.

'I think there is such a thing as the authority of, not reason with a capital R, but what we call intelligence,' he adds later. 'Nevertheless, I also agree with Dewey that it's always situated, it's never anonymous.'

And on that point, he is not about to change his mind.

Selected Bibliography

Mind, Language and Reality (Cambridge: Cambridge University Press, 1975)
Reason, Truth and History (Cambridge: Cambridge University Press, 1981)
Renewing Philosophy (Cambridge, MA: Harvard University Press, 1992)
Pragmatism: An Open Question (Cambridge, MA: Blackwell, 1995)
The Threefold Cord: Mind, Body, and World (New York: Columbia University Press, 1999)

Index